CITROËN 2CV

DIFFERENT IS EVERYTHING

MALCOLM BOBBITT

AMBERLEY

First published 2019

Amberley Publishing
The Hill, Stroud,
Gloucestershire, GL5 4EP

www.amberley-books.com

ISBN: 978 1 4456 8766 7 (print)
ISBN: 978 1 4456 8767 4 (ebook)

British Library Cataloguing in Publication Data.
A catalogue record for this book is available from the British Library.

Typeset in 10pt on 13pt Celeste.
Origination by Amberley Publishing.
Printed in the UK.

Contents

Introduction

The Deux Chevaux might easily have represented post-Second World War France. If hope of providing affordable, reliable and economical transport was a vital requirement, the demure corrugated-looking car seemingly bereft of any luxury fulfilled an important role.

In its idiosyncratic way the 2CV was, nevertheless, the essence of fruitfulness as anyone visiting or living in France in the fifties, sixties and seventies would have comprehended. Without sumptuous coachwork or fine upholstery, 2CVs going about their business were part of daily life. Farmers travelled across fields in them, took produce and livestock to market, and families relied upon them for shopping and the school run; the staple ingredient for the boulanger, épicier, poissonnier and boucher, the rippled Fourgonnette version was a familiar sight in any community. Seen hurrying as much as they could along the Routes Nationales just as frequently as pondering along rural byways, these distinctive and once ridiculed Citroëns had acquired a classless character. They were driven by students, teachers, university professors, factory workers, business leaders, bankers and politicians. Drive up to the entrance of the Ritz in the Place Vendôme and you'd receive the same welcome as would a president or royalty.

Wearing a nose-down attitude and often looking dishevelled through hard work, 2CVs emitted an immediately recognisable sound as their feebly powered air-cooled twin-cylinder engines fought to maintain momentum. When it came to riding cobbled streets or traversing the worst surfaces imaginable, nothing surpassed the Deux Chevaux with its unrivalled springing.

Conceived in the mid-1930s but not making its sensational debut until 1948, the 2CV was immediately derided for its parsimony. Hardly anyone, except for those who developed it in complete secrecy, thought it had a future. Dubbed the 'Umbrella on Four Wheels' because of its basic design, it attracted a raft of discourteous appellations, all of which added to the Citroën's mystique. France nevertheless took to the Deux Chevaux to make it a national institution.

In production for more than forty years, the 2CV's reputation travelled far beyond France. It was built in Britain as well as in Belgium and Portugal, and it outlived the model that was intended to replace it. In excess of 3 million 2CV saloons were built, but add to the number the commercial types and other variants that made it to production and the Deux Chevaux family swells to well over 8 million – all of which is an extraordinary feat for an unpretentious car that many commentators said would never sell!

Early 2CVs are recognisable by their corrugated bonnets, as demonstrated by this 1954 example. (Author)

Though late model 2CVs had slightly smoother styling, in this instance shown by the Charleston, they appeared remarkably similar to the original car. (Citroën)

Four Wheels under an Umbrella was the concept of the Deux Chevaux. This early advertising piece shows the car with its minimal appointment performing its role as essential family transport. (Citroën)

Acknowledgements

Thanks are extended to Citroën UK, especially Katie Read, Emma Gaffney and Mike Arnold for help in locating archive photographs; to Ragnar Ragnarson for allowing me to photograph his early 2CV and Ami 8; Henk Schuuring for the loan of early 2CV publicity material; Bill Wolf for his photographs, and the Citroën Car Club, in particular Brian Drummond, Richard Morris and David Conway.

Malcolm Bobbitt

1

Origins

'The car is not a luxury item but an essential implement of work' was André Citroën's proclamation in 1933 when declaring that motorised vehicles had become indispensable when transporting materials and produce. More than that, he decreed, the motor car presented itself as being a necessary form of personal transport for the population at large.

André Citroën's sentiments were not limited to the French motor industry: Morris in Britain had been building the Minor since 1929, while Standard marketed the Little Nine in 1932. Meanwhile, Herbert Austin's Seven made its debut in 1922, taking over the popular market from Citroën's small and ultra-basic two- and three-seater 5 hp of 1921. The design of the 5 hp went on to become the basis of Opel's very similar Laubfrosch, which was introduced three years later. Small utilitarian cars, a number being three-wheelers, emanated from Germany in the 1930s, and a plethora of tiny vehicles, including commercials, were being produced by Japan's motor industry.

When Citroën's Traction Avant was unveiled in 1934, along with Renault's Celtaquatre and Vivaquatre, together with Peugeot's 301, they were viewed as being for affluent motorists, and therefore unaffordable to the average Frenchman in menial employment or working on the land. André Citroën therefore perceived that a small and basically equipped car was needed; moreover, it had to be inexpensive, reliable and economical to run and maintain. *Le Patron*'s understanding of the social climate of France can be judged by him bringing mass production to the French auto industry in 1919.

The first cars to wear the Double Chevron insignia set a trend that was carried through to the late 1930s: the 1919 Type A was less expensive by far than its competitors, was economical to run and came fitted with accessories to include electric lighting and starting, a horn, full weather equipment and a spare wheel, thus ready to be driven away from the Citroën agent. It was the little 856cc 5 hp two-seater Type C of 1921, more often than not painted yellow to engender its *Petite Citron* epithet, which fully established Citroën in the people's car league. It was built until 1926 but André Citroën's mistake was not continuing with a frugal light car, thus leaving the market to Herbert Austin and his immortal Seven. Instead, Citroën believed that by employing the latest American methods he could build larger and better cars in greater numbers while selling them at the most competitive prices.

The Citroën marque can easily be claimed as being one of the most charismatic vehicles the global motor industry has witnessed. It has, throughout its century-long existence, catered for all customers, from peasant farmers to presidents. The range of cars over the

Citroën's engineering reputation was established on the design of its gear wheels, which featured the herringbone configuration, the double chevron becoming the firm's insignia. The gear installation depicted was photographed in a waterworks pumping station at Stockport in Cheshire in the early 1900s. (Citroën)

years have included the simplest of designs, as with the 'Little Lemon' rear-wheel drive Type C of the 1920s, to the pioneering Traction Avant of 1934 with its front-wheel drive, rakish styling and monocoque construction. Twenty-one years later came the technical complexity of the radical DS with its aerodynamic shape and use of hydropneumatics for suspension, braking and gear selection, a formula which summoned the stunning performance of the 1970s SM sports grand tourer. Not only did hydropneumatics play a part in the development of the 2CV, it appeared in embryonic form on the six-cylinder Traction Avant in 1954, a year ahead of the fully fledged system being employed on the DS. Always a subject of controversy and misunderstanding, it famously remained part of Citroën technology for more than six decades when specified for the CX in 1974 and thereafter the BX, Xantia, XM, C5 and C6 before being withdrawn in June 2017.

Mastermind of Automobiles Citroën was André Gustave Citroën, who was born in Paris in the early hours of 5 February 1878. Growing up in the final quarter of the nineteenth century, he witnessed the birth of the automobile and as a young man surely would have been aware of Louis Renault, who was almost a year older than himself, having been born on 12 February 1877. The two became possibly the greatest rivals in the history of motor manufacturing. Likewise, Peugeot, with its origins in the eighteenth century, would have been a household name as a pioneering constructor of automobiles.

Though André Citroën did not begin making motorcars bearing his name until 1919, he was by then well versed in the engineering and automobile industries, having graduated from the École Polytechnique in 1900 and, two years later, opened a workshop to fabricate

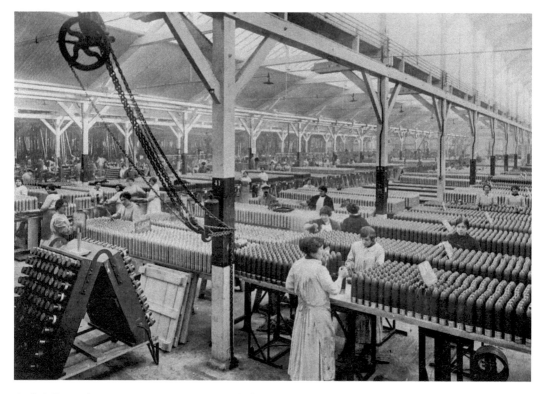

André Citroën's engineering prowess extended from gear-making to managing the car making business of Mors in 1908, and then to producing urgently needed ammunition for the First World War. This image shows the vast factory at Javel in Paris, where a total of 24 million shells were produced during the hostilities. After the war, the factory was turned over to building Citroën motor cars. (Citroën)

gearwheels using the Double Chevron pattern which he patented. Possibly the most famous attribution for the double helical gearwheel was its use in the ill-fated liner *Titanic*. In 1905 Citroën gained his experience in the motor industry when his engineering company, André Citroën et Cie, won a contract to build 500 engines for the Paris car maker Sizaire et Naudin. It was this venture that led him in 1908 to take on the responsibility of managing the Mors company, one of the oldest and most respected vehicle manufacturers in France. Founded in 1895, Mors not only amassed Grand Prix racing successes, its cars were considered as being the very best available. Amidst severe financial difficulties as a result of dwindling sales, Citroën was viewed as being the person to restructure the company and oversee the design and introduction of improved models and the installation of modern machinery, all of which helped to transform its fortunes. When, on the onset of hostilities in 1914, Citroën was mobilised as a reservist, he was to discover the plight of the French Army in respect of a serious shortage of shells. Though motor manufacturers had been enlisted to produce ammunition, the rate of supply was inadequate and made Citroën foresee that if France were to survive the war, a determined effort was needed to produce the required number of shells. In Citroën's typically meticulous manner, he used his contacts throughout industry to allow him to manufacture the urgently needed

The first Citroën was the Type A, which was built in 1919. An example was pictured outside the Javel factory entrance ten years later to celebrate a decade of Citroën car production. (Citroën)

ammunition in a purpose-built factory located at Javel on the bank of the River Seine in Paris. A former commune in the 15th arrondissement, it was built on market gardens and became the home of Automobiles Citroën in the wake of hostilities.

In view of *Le Patron*'s assertion in 1933, it could be presupposed that was the year of the 2CV's conception. Other than his loose forecast, nothing about the Deux Chevaux was planned; no drawings existed, and furthermore André Citroën did not live to see his prophecy materialise. While the eventual Deux Chevaux carried the double chevron insignia and exhibited the qualities of the fertile minds of those engineers Citroën had recruited, it was a car and a success story that he could never have possibly imagined. Nevertheless, it would surely have satisfied his quest to build affordable cars for mass markets. There is no doubt whatsoever that Citroën admired the business ethics of Henry Ford, whom he visited in Detroit in 1912, and it was his mass production methods which Citroën introduced at Javel in 1919, thus bringing this now familiar technique to Europe.

The notion of a true people's car had, in fact, been investigated by the Michelin Tyre Company as early as 1922, twelve years before it acquired Automobiles Citroën in December 1934 following the car maker's financial collapse. Citroën's difficulties were mainly attributed to the huge outlay and intense development involved in designing, developing and the rush to put into mass production the Traction Avant. With Citroën afraid that he would be beaten by other manufacturers in getting such a car into production, not only was the Traction Avant leaving the assembly lines before all the many teething problems were ironed out, his health suffered from the severe strain. He was already in a fragile state as he fought stomach cancer, and the aggravation of both perfecting the front-wheel drive system and finding the crucial finance to keep the company afloat contributed to his death in July 1935 at the age of fifty-seven. Hence, he was denied the knowledge his company had produced a truly pioneering motor car that would influence motor design for decades to come.

The 2CV's predecessors included the Austin Seven and, depicted here, the Citroën 5 hp of 1921, which was marketed as a popular type of vehicle. This two-seater was joined by a three-seater and was often painted yellow, hence its *Petite Citron* epithet. (Citroën)

The 5 hp, seen here in its popular yellow hue and being driven by a young woman, was a big success for Citroën. A mistake was that Citroën did not replace it when the model was withdrawn in 1926, and it would be more than twenty years before the company produced another 'people's car', the 2CV. (Author's collection)

Michelin's desire to see a 'people's car' was inspired by a survey which revealed there being a car for every ten inhabitants in America in the early 1920s, a far cry from the 1 in 150 in France, which was still considered to be an agrarian country. Needless to say, Michelin would not have cared whether any one of the 'big four' car makers, Citroën, Panhard, Peugeot or Renault, had taken up the challenge of designing such a vehicle, as long as it used Michelin tyres. The idea for a small utilitarian car was again considered in 1934 when Pierre Michelin, the son of Édouard Michelin, who with his brother André founded the company in 1899, ordered that a testbed be constructed to assess the viability of a lightweight tyre for a rudimentary experimental vehicle he was considering.

It is the Michelin link that is vital in the history of the 2CV since the initiative that made the car a possibility stemmed from the formative days of the tyre maker's acquisition of Automobiles Citroën in December 1934, only months after the introduction of the Traction Avant. The collapse of Automobiles Citroën came about when, earlier that year, Jean Ostheimer, the director of Compagnie Franco-Américane des Jante en Bois, a relatively small creditor being a supplier of steering wheels, filed a winding-up petition in the French commercial court. The result was catastrophic for Citroën, which showed it owing 475 million francs, 60 million of which was owed to Michelin, who ultimately took on the responsibility of the car manufacturer.

Michelin could easily have put a restraint on Citroën's widely publicised adventurous design and engineering undertakings. Instead, the opposite route was taken whereby the design of the Traction Avant was perfected and its post-production problems in terms of reliability were rectified. Significantly, Michelin endorsed Citroën's radical thinking to

A Citroën B2 in cutaway form at the 1923 Paris Motor Show. (Citroën)

Citroën built rear-drive cars until 1939, this being a Rosalie from 1934, the year that the Traction Avant was introduced. Note the double chevron on the radiator grille. (Author)

include the technically advanced proposals for the Traction Avant's eventual replacement. At the helm of Citroën, the two-man team comprising Pierre Michelin and Pierre-Jules Boulanger managed the business while collaborating on the technical interests of the two firms. Pierre Michelin oversaw Citroën's finances, administration and commercial affairs while Pierre-Jules Boulanger, a trained architect who in the wake of the First World War had joined Michelin to supervise the extending of its Clermont-Ferrand factory and headquarters, was responsible for managing the day-to-day running of Citroën's factories and the accomplishments of its experimental department.

Pierre Boulanger, who was born on 10 March 1885, might never have pursued an engineering career had he not forsaken his youthful studies in fine art to seek work in the USA in 1908 after completing his national service, which was then compulsory for all young Frenchmen. He took several jobs, from being a ranch-hand to driving trams in San Francisco, and later joined a firm of architects as a draftsman where he excelled in his duties. His experience in architecture prompted him to move to Vancouver in Canada where he set up a house building company. His business as a house constructor was short-lived owing to the outbreak of war in August 1914 when he returned to France to join the same military unit, the 25th Balloon Observation Battalion, where he had completed his national service. In November 1914 he was reassigned to the French Army Air Corps – Service Aéronautique – specialising in aerial photography for which he was decorated for bravery, his awards including the Légion d'Honneur, the Belgian Croix de Guerre and the

André and Giorgina Citroën pictured in the early 1920s. André Citroën's penchant for gambling was well known and he was a regular visitor to the casino at Deauville. He was also a skilled publicist. (Citroën)

honorary Order of the British Empire. During his war service, Boulanger was reunited with his friend Marcel Michelin, whose uncle Édouard persuaded him not to return to America or Canada after the Armistice, but to work for Michelin.

In addition to planning forthcoming models, including a front-wheel drive van, which emerged pre-war as the TUB and post-war as the characteristically corrugated Type H, Pierre Boulanger was insistent on there being a *Toute Petite Voiture* of an inexpensive and utilitarian nature to afford minimal motoring for the rural French. The TPV, as it was code-named, was to be without any pretensions or preconceived values – indeed, it should embody the most creative thinking. Boulanger had noticed that in the provinces French farmers usually attended markets by either bicycle or horse and cart, but seldom by motor vehicle. He maintained that a simple, go-anywhere and easily maintained car would, as well as being advantageous to these communities, bring much needed revenue to Citroën. He revealed his ideas in October 1935 which called for a 'peasant's car' capable of accommodating four people, having a top speed of 70–80 km/h on a level road, an average fuel consumption of 5 litres per 100 km and selling for around 5,000 francs – or no more than a third of the price of a Traction Avant. The parameters were based on an investigation conducted to assess what sort of vehicle was favoured, and it was only after the results were analysed in depth that Michelin's directors gave the go-ahead for the TPV to be developed.

The substance of the TPV mirrored some of those principles expressed by Pierre Michelin in 1934 when arranging the testing of a lightweight tyre. This was attested by Boulanger, who fine-tuned the specification by reducing the top speed to 60 km/h, which helped to improve the fuel consumption to 3 litres/100 km. Both his and Michelin's convictions about a minimal car would have been influenced by Fiat's development of the diminutive Cinquecento, which made its first outing in prototype form in early October 1934, and which was introduced to the Italian market in 1936, a couple of months after making its debut in France as the Simca Cinq. And surely news of Porsche's Type 32 for NSU, arguably a forerunner to the VW Beetle, caused interest at Javel. Not least, it was anticipated that Renault was planning a small rear-engined people's car, the 4CV prototype emerging in 1942 and coining the 'Little Pat of Butter' epithet owing to its diminutive size and shape. Looking at that prototype design today, it is remarkable how alike it is to the Fiat 500 Nuova, which was introduced in 1957.

Boulanger's 1934 design brief was not universally admired. Maurice Broglie, head of Citroën's experimental department – the Bureau d'Études – considered it to be unworkable and impossible to produce, but Boulanger was adamant about its possibilities and stipulated a long list of obligations. Broglie, despite his reservations about the project, got on with the matter and commissioned the Bureau d'Études to begin work producing ideas for prototype cars.

Anyone looking at Boulanger's demands might easily concur with Broglie's opinion. A motorised cart so uncomplicated it could be driven by anyone with little or no driving experience might well be considered to be impractical. That it was essentially 'four wheels beneath an umbrella' gives the clue as to the TPV's austere characteristics, but combining this with the requirement to carry up to four passengers in comfort over the poorest roads, even crossing ploughed fields, added to the challenge. When adding constraints such as that the vehicle be capable of transporting a basket of eggs without one of them being broken, or that it should be able to accommodate two people in addition to 50 kg of potatoes and a cask of wine, the degree of scepticism can be appreciated. Moreover, Boulanger gave little thought as to the TPV's styling; he viewed this as being largely immaterial as long as durability and reliability were paramount since even modest repair costs would be unacceptable to the class of customer he had in mind for the car.

Work on the proposed TPV was conducted in complete secrecy at three locations, one being in a corner of the Paris workshops that were once part of the Mors premises in the Rue de Théatre, near to the Quai de Javel factory but sufficiently isolated as to go undetected. Another was at Levallois, a suburb of Paris, in a factory once home to Clément bicycles which André Citroën acquired in the early 1920s to extend car production when the Javel works were operating at full capacity. The third was 130 km west of Paris at La Ferté-Vidame near Dreux, where Citroën had established a purpose-built test track. Located within a vast and wooded estate that had been purchased by Pierre Boulanger on behalf of the Michelin family, the security of the facility was such that only test drivers and key personnel knew of its existence.

With Maurice Broglie having overall supervision over the TPV project, Maurice Sainturat, who had produced the Traction Avant's engine and transmission, was given responsibility for engine design. Chief engineer was André Lefebvre, a protégé of Gabriel Voisin who had gone to Renault before being invited by André Citroën to perfect the Traction Avant's

Above left: André Lefebvre was André Citroën's right-hand man, having been hired to develop the Traction Avant, after which he was put in charge of engineering the 2CV. (Citroën)

Above right: Flaminio Bertoni was employed by André Citroën to style the Traction Avant, and afterwards he was responsible for the 2CV and later the DS and Ami 6. (Citroën)

The first of Citroën's front-wheel drive cars was the Traction Avant, which was introduced in 1934. Incorporating chassis-less construction as well as being mass-produced, it set automotive design for decades ahead. This early example is being tested by *The Motor*. (*The Motor*)

engineering and construction. André Lefebvre was born at Louvres to the north of Paris on 14 August 1894. He studied at the École Supérieure d'Aéronautique at Montmartre in the French capital, where he gained an engineering diploma in 1914 and joined Gabriel Voisin on 1 March 1916. Initially working on military aircraft, Lefebvre's talents were put to use designing very advanced luxury automobiles as well some of the most powerful racing cars motor sport had witnessed. He also competed in motor sport, racing at the highest level and driving for the Voisin team to take fifth place in the 1923 Grand Prix de l'Automobile Club de France, held at Tours, when at the wheel of a 2-litre, six-cylinder machine. Not only was the Voisin exceptionally aerodynamic, it employed a monocoque body that was built of almost entirely light alloy which Lefebvre had helped to design. He also raced at Montlhéry, where he often involved himself in high-speed, long-distance endurance runs that were all part of testing new cars to extreme limits. It is not unreasonable to assume that André Citroën would have been aware of Lefebvre's skills since Automobiles Citroën became famous for staging a series of sensational endurance records with its Rosalie models in association with the oil company Yacco at Montlhéry between 1931 and 1936.

With his team in place, Boulanger expected the car to be ready in time for the 1940 Paris Motor Show. There is evidence that Maurice Broglie's reservations about the 2CV's design brief was further aggravated by Lefebvre's appointment, especially as Pierre Boulanger had given Lefebvre freedom to do whatever he thought necessary to satisfy the design edict. Interestingly, whereby most car makers' smaller and more economical models were effectively scaled down versions of larger cars, Lefebvre took the more unconventional direction by employing a dedicated approach towards a simple car offering as much interior space as a full-size model.

Following the financial collapse of Citroën, and the company being acquired by Michelin, Pierre Boulanger was placed in charge of day-to-day running. He oversaw the perfection of the Traction Avant after the car had been introduced before development was complete, and in 1936 set out the design parameters for the 2CV. (Citroën)

When Citroën resumed car production after the Second World War, it concentrated on front-wheel drive. Traction Avant models continued to be built until 1957, though stopped in 1955 in Britain, and therefore influenced some of the 2CV's engineering. The Traction Avant depicted is the six-cylinder 15-6. (Citroën)

André Lefebvre's engineering prowess dictated the TPV's mechanical blueprint. Foremost, by placing the centre of gravity as far forward and as low as possible in the interest of maximum stability, it would have front-wheel drive with the engine and transmission placed ahead of the front wheels. Steering would be by rack and pinion with 2.3 turns of the steering wheel lock-to-lock to afford the most positive handling. The body of the car would not be load bearing, and therefore would perform Boulanger's 'umbrella' role. It would be simply affixed to a rigid pontoon-like platform to which the wheels and suspension would be attached to front and rear tubular cross members. The suspension itself would afford the softest ride possible when the car rode over rough surfaces. This was achieved by having leading and trailing curved and swinging axle arms to provide exceptionally long up and down travel of the independent torsion bar system, interconnected front-to-rear on both sides of the vehicle. A vast number of ideas were considered, not least a ladder frame chassis comprising aluminium tubes which served as cooling ducts for the engine.

André Lefebvre's experience working with Gabriel Voisin in respect to aeroplane design had given him a proficiency in the use of weight saving techniques, especially when employing aluminium, a material with which he was familiar. There is little surprise, therefore, that corrugated light alloy in the form of duralinox and magnesium to afford torsional stiffness was specified for the TPV's floorplan and bolt-on body panels. For the doors and roof, the latter extending down to the tail, use of waxed canvas helped keep weight to a minimum. The interior was bereft of any refinement and instrumentation; hammock-type seats followed aircraft practice, and glass for the windows was abandoned

Ideas for the 2CV centred around a minimal car that would be inexpensive in both purchase and running costs, and that had to be easy to maintain. One of the cars that Pierre Boulanger studied was the tiny Fiat 500, which made its debut in 1936. The car featured a four-cylinder water-cooled engine with its radiator placed aft and above it. Behind the Fiat is a Citroën Traction Avant, a British-built pre-war Light 15 model. (Author's collection)

Part of the Mors premises in Paris at the Rue de Théatre became the drawing office and design hub used to create the Deux Chevaux in secrecy. It was conveniently close to Citroën's Javel headquarters but sufficiently far away to enjoy isolation from prying eyes. Note the headlight units on the table, which appear to be the same as the single affair fitted to the prototype car. (Citroën)

in favour of plastic. A battery was considered unnecessary since a single headlight on the vehicle's off-side was powered by a dynamo in the style of that found on motorcycles, and hand-starting the engine was in preference to employing a starter motor, the latter flying in the face of Citroën's principles when offering the Type A in 1919.

On Pierre Boulanger's directive in 1937 to construct 250 prototype TPVs over a period of two years, countless problems were encountered. Welding the joints of the floorpans of the first examples caused difficulties, especially so when it was discovered that the light alloy material rapidly disintegrated when exposed to flames caused by a spark from an electrical short circuit. More troubles were revealed as cars began to split apart under torsional stress. Exacerbating the complications, the suspension was so soft that vehicles sank to the ground when fully laden. Maintaining an even keel when braking, or carrying a heavy load at the rear, such as the all-important sack of potatoes, took enormous efforts to achieve, while just as worrying was the fuel consumption, which was far in excess of Boulanger's expectations. Not least of the concerns, engine power output was feeble beyond measure.

A horizontally opposed twin-cylinder 375cc water-cooled engine was originally specified for the TPV, the radiator being mounted aft and above it in similar fashion to that seen on the Fiat Topolino. For all Boulanger's demands that the TPV be easy to maintain, test

Above left: The prototype 2CV, which was intended to be introduced in 1940. It was so bereft of equipment, a single headlight was considered to be adequate. The car was without an electric starter, hence the starting handle, while a single windscreen wiper sufficed. Windows were made from a plastic material and those in the front doors had an opening flap; the roof was made from waxed canvas and rolled fully back to the rear glass, and the same material was used for the roll-up boot cover. The bodywork was formed from a light alloy, the bonnet being ribbed to afford strengthening. (Citroën)

Above right: The prototype 2CV featured a 375cc water-cooled flat-twin engine, with the radiator positioned aft. A number of problems were experienced with the design and ultimately an air-cooled 375cc flat-twin was designed. (Citroën)

drivers found it necessary to remove one of the front wings when topping up the engine oil. Furthermore, without even a fuel tank dipstick, there was a high risk of running out of petrol. The nightmarish situation worsened when starting the engine became impossible in cold weather.

Compounding the difficulties, the steering wheel along with the brake, clutch and accelerator pedals were poorly positioned, and the hand brake ineffective. Vision through the windows became all but impossible when static electricity caused dust to collect on the plastic; the hood let in rain and draughts; and with there being no heater the TPV presented a miserable form of transport in cold weather. Despite feverish efforts to have the TPV perfected for 1940, in reality it was in no state of readiness for production. Nevertheless, Pierre Boulanger, having tested a substantial number of prototypes in the spring of 1939, ordered that assembly of pre-production TPVs should commence at the Levallois factory.

Ironically, the saviour of the TPV was the onset of hostilities in September 1939. The Paris Motor Show was cancelled, the northern half of France was in a state of military occupation and Citroën was effectively under German command. Production of civilian cars was halted while the Quai de Javel factory was given over to constructing lorries for the German war effort. Pierre Boulanger, who steadfastly refused to co-operate with the Wehrmacht and condoned his workers' activities which hindered production, immediately instructed that all the prototype TPVs be hidden, both at La Ferté-Vidame and at Levallois. Before the war Boulanger ordered the prototypes be destroyed, but four escaped this fate having been concealed so well they remained undiscovered for some three decades. A fifth prototype spent many years at Michelin's Clermont-Ferrand factory serving as a pick-up truck, its origins and importance having all that time gone unrecognised.

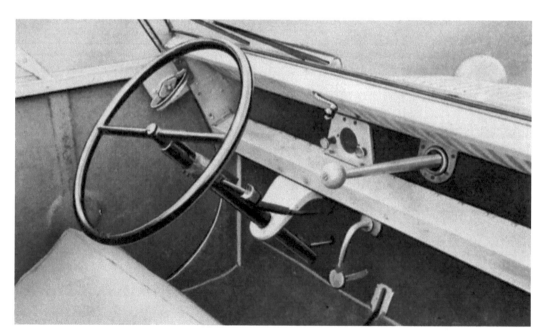

The prototype 2CV's basic interior. The gear lever sprouting from the bulkhead remained in modified form to production. (Citroën)

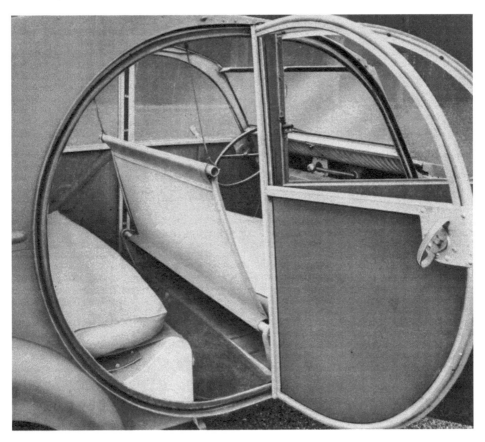

The prototype 2CV's hammock seats followed aircraft practice and afforded surprising comfort despite their simple design. The rear seats were also basic but nevertheless provided comfort. (Citroën)

The 2CV was designed to seat four passengers in comfort, with the suspension being compliant enough for a basket of eggs to be transported over rough ground without a single one breaking. The basic shape of the prototype was carried over through production to 1990. (Citroën)

Many problems were experienced in perfecting the 2CV's design ahead of the car's anticipated 1940 introduction. In 1937, Pierre Boulanger ordered the construction of 250 prototype vehicles for testing purposes, but at the onset of hostilities in 1939 he ordered they be destroyed to save them from going into enemy hands. Despite Boulanger's orders five cars escaped their fate, and three of them are seen here when their hiding place was discovered post-war. Interestingly, the middle car has twin headlights when only a single type was specified, on the car's off-side. (Citroën)

The testing of prototype 2CVs was undertaken at Citroën's test track at La Ferté-Vidame between Paris and Le Mans. Hidden in the French countryside in the confines of a chateau, the track was known only to the personnel involved with the car's development. This photograph was taken in 1939 despite a strict ban on all photography at the site. The image shows three prototypes being tested. Note the centrally positioned headlamp on the lead car. (Citroën)

In truth, the TPV was so primitive and feebly powered that it would surely have deterred the very customers Pierre Boulanger had envisaged would buy it. The German occupation of France therefore gave time for Citroën's Bureau d'Études to secretly perfect what became the Mk ll – essentially the 2CV blueprint. Flaminio Bertoni, who had sculpted the Traction Avant, was assigned to giving the TPV a softer styling profile, and in the process included a centrally positioned headlight. Light gauge steel was used for the construction of the body and chassis, the latter to André Lefebvre's design, which employed coil springs housed within horizontal tubes attached to the underside of the platform in place of the torsion bars. Though the suspension obviated any pitching, inertia dampers fitted to the ends of the axle arms adjacent to the wheels honed the ride quality. In the process of designing the modified system, Paul Magès, Citroën's hydraulics specialist, devised a hydropneumatic suspension system for the 2CV, which was also tried for the H Van in its development. The system's complexity made it too expensive for a minimal car, and indeed the Type H commercial, and was instead adopted for the DS of 1955, though the 1954 six-cylinder Traction was used as a testbed for it, albeit on the rear axle only.

Flaminio Bertoni – who is today celebrated as being the styling genius he was, but was for far too long ignored in France for his outstanding work commensurate with the most recognised designers on both sides of the Atlantic – was born in northern Italy on 10 January 1903. The son of a stonemason, he commenced work at the age of fourteen in an aircraft factory as an apprentice carpenter. Rather than aircraft, his interests lay in automobile design and construction, and after qualifying as a sheet metal worker he taught himself draughtsmanship and sculpturing, for which he had an inbuilt gift. He lacked formal qualifications however, and at the age of twenty-three went to Paris, where he worked as an artist, book illustrator and sculptor. When his talents were discovered by André Citroën, he was invited to join his company, initially assisting in the styling of models. His skills being recognised, he gradually took over the responsibility of all interior and exterior car designs, staying with Citroën until his death in 1964.

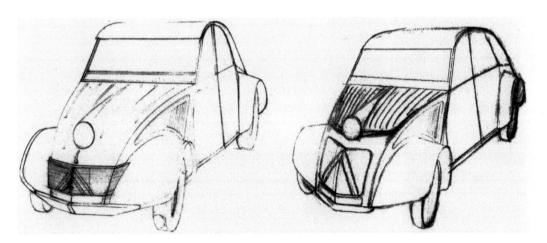

The 2CV's many teething troubles, and not least its ultra-primitive design, meant that had the 1940 Paris Motor Show gone ahead it would have been unready. The hostilities gave time for the design to be re-appraised and shown here are Flaminio Bertoni's initial re-styling proposals. The war years also gave time for newly appointed Walter Becchia to re-design the car's engine. (Citroën)

Instead of a single headlight on the 2CV's offside, Bertoni proposed a faired-in cyclops lamp, which he ultimately changed for twin headlights. (Citroën)

Joining the Bureau d'Études from Talbot-Lago, Walter Becchia, in the space of a week, redesigned Maurice Sainturat's engine, adopting air instead of water cooling. Becchia, like Bertoni, was born in northern Italy in 1896 and was thus seven years his senior. He began his automotive career with Fiat, helping to design the engine fitted to the Fiat 804 which won both the French and Italian Grand Prix in 1922. Moving to England, where he joined Sunbeam-Talbot-Darracq, he designed the straight-six engine Sir Henry Segrave used to take victory in the 1923 French Grand Prix. Adopting French citizenship in the 1930s, he was recruited by Pierre Boulanger to succeed Maurice Sainturat following his retirement. Becchia was an ardent devotee of the air-cooled engine and persuaded Lefebvre and Boulanger as to its virtues, including the use of aluminium for non-wearing parts. It proved to be a masterpiece of design: compact, lightweight and precision engineered, it weighed 90 pounds, which was barely half the weight of a cast-iron engine of comparative output and size. Becchia's design included attaching the cooling fan to the nose of the crankshaft and installing an oil cooler in the airflow to afford an optimal operating temperature as long as the engine was running. Testing the engine involved running it at full throttle for days on end without failure. Another of Becchia's ideas was to do away with the normal distributor and instead install contact breakers on the end of the camshaft, which in turn provided a spark at both plugs for every revolution of the crankshaft. The car was still without a starter motor, there being a pull device behind the steering wheel; when secretaries at Citroën were invited to test it, and damaged their fingernails in the process, Boulanger immediately sanctioned the fitting of an electric self-starter.

Walter Becchia proposed that a four-speed gearbox replace the original three-speed affair, this meeting with Boulanger's firm refusal. Becchia's obstinacy matched Boulanger's stubbornness, which resulted in the eventual compromise of an overdrive, though the fourth gear position was not displayed on the gear selector, its presence denoted simply by the letter 'S' indicating 'Supermultiple'.

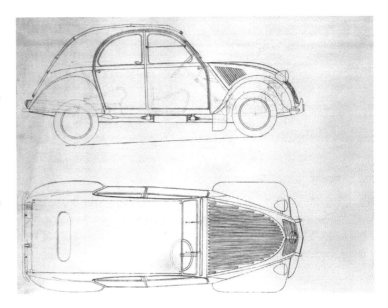

Nearly there: apart from some very minor design tweaks, this is Flaminio Bertoni's design for the pre-production 2CV. Glass has replaced the plastic windows, twin windscreen wipers are fitted and the car has two headlights. The body shape has been smoothed but final touches await the rear wings. (Citroën)

In its new shape, which by 1945 resembled the definitive 2CV, pre-production cars were subjected to constant testing at La Ferté-Vidame with Pierre Boulanger taking personal supervision, even to the extent of driving them at weekends to check on fuel consumption. Many modifications, including the new platform, bodywork, starter motor, glass windows replacing plastic, two headlamps instead of the cyclops affair and a rudimentary heater, made the car considerably heavier and more refined than originally specified. Boulanger's insistence about paring weight to a minimum was largely marginalised when, at the 1946 Paris Motor Show, Renault revealed its four-door and four-cylinder rear-engined 4CV, two years ahead of the 2CV's introduction. The 4CV in its production form had lost its minimalist 'pat of butter' appearance and was set for a long production run, being replaced by the rear-engined Dauphine in 1956. From Citroën's establishment it had always rivalled Renault, their main factories being on opposite banks of the River Seine. In Britain, too, the two firms carried on their rivalry to a much lesser degree, and like Citroën at Slough, Renault too had a British assembly plant, at Acton on the Western Avenue, in which to produce vehicles for the United Kingdom and British Commonwealth countries. It was there that the 4CV, with its slant toward British customer preferences, was built in modest numbers.

When the 2CV was unveiled on 7 October 1948 at the Grand Palais d'Exposition it had already created acrimony among Citroën agents who, appalled at what they saw in respect of the car's shape and minimal specification, were convinced it would not sell. Their concerns were highlighted when an opportunist photo-journalist from the French newspaper *La Presse* managed to break the security cordon around the normally highly protected grounds surrounding the La Ferté-Vidame test track and photographed an experimental car, and one that did not even depict the definitive design. Though Citroën had thus far successfully kept the development of the TPV secret, the tell-tale image emblazoned across the newspaper's pages summoned much derision as to the car maker's intentions. Boulanger, being fully committed to the 2CV's merits, resolutely rebuffed the

Flaminio Bertoni's final outline for the Deux Chevaux. Essentially, the styling remained throughout production. (Citroën)

agents' demands to reshape the car to make it appear more acceptable. Their protests were in vain, but in the event they needn't have worried because, despite the media ridicule, not only had 1¼ million visitors to the Grand Palais rushed to Citroën's stand to get a glimpse of the car, but thousands of orders were taken, even though it would be some seven months before the 2CV entered production. Chaos reigned as visitors unsuccessfully tried to open the bonnets of the show cars, which were sealed for the good reason that they were empty since the engines were under final development. The suspension was also of great curiosity, and security personnel were called to stop visitors trying to rock the 2CVs up and down to see just how effective the springing was.

Though Pierre Boulanger had the satisfaction of seeing the 2CV's unveiling and eventual early production, he did not live to see the true success of the car since he was killed in December 1950 when travelling between Paris and Clermont-Ferrand, driving an experimental Traction Avant. The cause of the accident was never known: it could have been because he was in a hurry, or through tiredness or even possibly that he was not familiar with the experimental car. There is a sequence of tragedies here since Pierre Michelin died in a motor accident on 29 December 1937 when he hit a patch of black ice on the Route Nationale 7 between Briare and Montargis. Fate again struck when Pierre Lefaucheux, the brain behind the new cars at Renault, died on 11 February 1955 when his car, a Renault Frégate, skidded after hitting ice on the road at Saint-Dizier and overturned, his suitcase placed on the car's rear seat being flung forwards and hitting him on the back of his head.

At 185,000 old francs (approximately £175) the 2CV was viewed as an extremely attractive proposition when likened to the comparatively priced ultra-basic two-seaters such as the flat-twin water-cooled Rovin or the like of the twin-cylinder two-stroke Boitel and the air-cooled flat-four Dolo. Those customers who adventurously placed orders for the 2CV at the Paris Motor Show faced a long wait before taking delivery. Production did not commence until 23 June 1949, and by the end of the year fewer than 900 examples had left Levallois, by which time the price had escalated to 228,000 francs (around £215).

Levallois was chosen to produce the 2CV owing to Javel being committed to production of the Traction Avant. The factory dated from 1893, when it was home to the Clément bicycle manufactured by Adolphe Clément, his AC initials being superimposed on steel

The 2CV was announced at the 1948 Paris Motor Show and was the cause of much debate regarding its design and frugal specification. The car's suspension was of interest and visitors tried rocking the car on its soft springing. Despite onlookers wanting to see the car's motor, the bonnets were sealed since the engine design was incomplete. There still remained work to be done before the car could enter production. (Citroën)

bicycle wheels along the frontage of the premises. Elsewhere on the building 'Usine A Clément' laid claim to the building's provenance. In addition to bicycles, Adolphe Clément ventured into building motor vehicles to become one of the most important figures in the formative years of the French motor industry, and one of the largest car makers in Europe with the Levallois factory employing some 1,500 personnel. When Clément retired in 1914, the company he established went into decline without his vibrant personality. By 1922 it was all over for the firm and the Levallois factory was acquired by André Citroën, who utilised it to build the 5 hp Type C. With the demise of the Type C the works were given over to a diverse number of purposes, not least the manufacture of accessories such as wheels and other components, but also for the construction of the Citroën Kegresse, the cross-country half-track vehicles which were utilised for a variety of uses including farming and industry as well as being employed by the military. These vehicles saw service around the world when engaged on expeditions across the Sahara Desert, exploration of darkest Africa and a route crossing the Himalayas to reach Peking. When putting the 2CV into production, Levallois was the option chosen.

2

Early Production

The weeks in the run-up to the 1948 Paris Motor Show, which opened on 7 October at the Grand Palais, constituted, according to the newspapers and the motoring press, a dreary and uncertain time. Even the prospect of the show itself, usually a glittering occasion with new cars being the talk of cafés and social columns in the likes of *Paris Match*, was seemingly unable to raise morale and any hope of better times in the wake of the hostilities which had ravaged France and its neighbours.

The 2CV unveiled at the 1948 Paris Motor Show; Pierre Boulanger (right) presents the car to President Vincent Auriol. (Citroën)

The Friday 1 October editorial of *The Autocar*, normally optimistic and setting a bristling scene, was filled with pessimism when it likened a car designer to 'a research worker locked in a closet waiting for the political and cultural scene to awaken, and the factories would hum in tune with meaningful production'. The editorial continued: 'Conditions would be met with the characteristically Gallic shrug of the shoulders signifying there would not be any prospect of interesting new cars.'

At least France, unlike Britain, which did not resume showcasing its motor industry until 1948, had been staging post-war motor shows despite that country's dire economy and absence of resources along with severe shortages of raw materials with which to recommence manufacturing. The occupation of France had left the nation in a state whereby factories had been plundered or destroyed by bombing raids, and therefore commodities including steel and fuel, in addition to components such as tyres, were strictly rationed.

In its same 1 October edition, *The Autocar* presented a two-page feature outlining the new models that were scheduled to make their appearance at the Grand Palais. The Simca Six, mechanically similar to the Fiat 500B Topolino but more modern in appearance with its headlights faired into the front wings, presented a challenger to the Renault 4CV, which had been unveiled two years before. Peugeot, too, was offering quantity production with its 1.3-litre 203, which took styling cues from American cars. Panhard also got a mention with its 610cc flat-twin engined Dyna, as did Citroën's Traction Avant four- and six-cylinder cars. Though such vehicles as the Rovin minicar and its rivals the Boitel, Aerocarene and Julien were reviewed, there was no mention of the 2CV.

It was not until the following week that *The Autocar* and its rival *The Motor* excitedly enthused over the unveiling of the 2CV, which they rightly claimed as being the sensation of the Salon. Possibly, but unlikely, the motoring press was caught on the hop, especially as it was reported that Citroën had revealed to a startled public that the 375cc two-cylinder economy car had front-wheel drive with all 'the severe practicality of approach of the wartime Jeep'. In other words, it was capable of going anywhere, even over ploughed fields, just as Pierre Boulanger had decreed. Its agility, the report continued, was courtesy of the spindly wheels, light weight and the most forgiving suspension system, the operation of which Citroën refused to reveal at the time of the motor show. Other contemporary reports in the motoring media mentioned, but almost sidelined, the fact that the Deux Chevaux, which created so much attention, was without an engine beneath the corrugated bonnet. Of significant interest, though, was the mention that during the car's development, hydraulic suspension, in the form of hydropneumatics, had been considered, this having given way to the mechanical interconnected springs housed in tubes beneath the chassis.

It should be explained that the hydropneumatic suspension trialled for the 2CV and the Type H Van, and which was eventually fitted to the 1954 Traction Avant six-cylinder car as a testbed ahead of being specified for the 1955 DS19, has long been considered a Citroën masterpiece of engineering. Though Citroën made such a system work – even to the extent that it was used in later years by Rolls-Royce as a means of applying self-levelling to the otherwise conventionally sprung Silver Shadow and its Bentley T sister car in 1965 – its ideals extend far into the annals of automotive history. Several car makers comprehended the practicalities of hydropneumatics, as did aircraft

A pre-production 2CV on test in September 1948. This is one of several images taken on the occasion of the Deux Chevaux being photographed for the first time for official publicity purposes. The car is not quite in its definitive state since the lower edges of the rear wings have a slight concave shape. (Citroën)

Another view of the pre-production 2CV. The photograph sees Marcel Chinon, who co-ordinated the 2CV design programme, driving, while next to him is Madame Gaulon, who was Pierre Boulanger's secretary. Sitting in the rear is Jacques Duclos, who undertook a market research survey to establish the type of car French motorists wanted, and nearest the camera is Jean Cadiou of Citroën's Bureau d'Études. The upward curve on the lower edge of the rear wing is clearly visible. (Citroën)

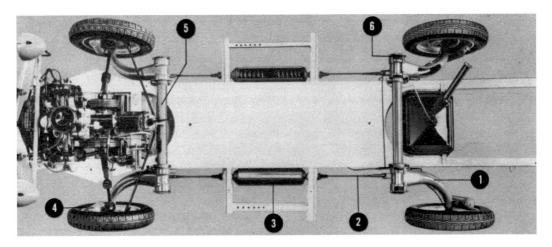

The 2CV's suspension, showing 1) curved axle arms, 2) interconnecting suspension rods, 3) suspension cylinders, 4) inertia dampers, 5) torsion bars, and 6) friction disc. (Citroën)

manufacturers when designing undercarriage systems, but none could perfect it. The idea of fluid under pressure being distributed from a central reservoir to spheres attached to the wheels and chassis (*suspension hydraulique*) was actually conceived and patented by Renault in 1908 as described in a feature appearing at that time in the French journal *La Vie Automobile*.

There is little wonder that the French were bemused by the 2CV's appearance with its corrugated bonnet, four doors and simple lightly cushioned hammock-type seats supported on rubber bands stretched over the tubular frames. Moreover, the idea of a full-length canvas roof opening to below the rear screen, while the lower section meeting the rear bumper could be rolled up to give access to the boot, was seen as outright austerity. Compared to other economy cars, including the genre of minimalist minicars, the 2CV with its promised 375cc air-cooled flat twin motor was the smallest engined vehicle at the time. Getting the Deux Chevaux, enshrouded with sheets tied at each of the four corners around the bumpers to hide the treasured design beneath, into La Grand Palais proved to be a major exercise. Unloaded from a wagon outside the premises, the veiled vehicle was, courtesy of many willing hands, manhandled to Citroën's stand. Once there, it was lifted into place upon its dais, every precaution being taken to conceal the car beneath the sheeting. Nevertheless, tantalising glimpses were afforded of the wheels and sections of the bodywork.

Despite its unveiling at the Paris show, the 2CV was conspicuous by its absence at the London Motor Show, which opened at Earls Court on 27 October, even though Citroën Cars Ltd with its manufacturing base at Slough was a highly respected company. Renault, nevertheless, scored by exhibiting a left-hand drive version of its 4CV in a cutaway format designed to reveal its rear-engine layout and independent coil suspension. Intriguingly, the latest incarnation of the Rovin minicar, which had been introduced in France earlier in 1948, was displayed with its slab-sided 'loaf of bread' styling and 425cc rear-engine layout. The car's importers probably envisaged few sales, and in any event did not have a right-hand drive model to display.

The 2CV's 375cc air-cooled twin-cylinder engine mated with a four-speed gearbox and showing the drive shafts. The cylinder heads are so finely engineered that they are without gaskets. (Citroën)

The subject of minicars was generously investigated by Gordon Wilkins in the 10 December edition of *The Autocar* when he described them as being akin to household utensils, 'stark as lawn mowers and functional as wheelbarrows'. In this category came the Bond Mark A three-wheeler built by Sharp's Commercials in Lancashire, the aforementioned Rovin and, in his opinion, the 2CV. In truth the Citroën, which wasn't a minicar, was all the more sophisticated and cleverly engineered: not only did it offer four seats instead of the normally expected two, albeit they were secured on the platform by pegs for easy removal, but the four doors were without hinges since they were simply secured by interlocking sections in the centre pillars. The same applied to the bonnet, which in the open position could be slid away from the scuttle. Little changed throughout more than forty years of production: the bonnets on the last cars were affixed in the same way, though hinges were added to the front doors when the design changed from the original 'suicide' rear-hung type to being suspended on the front pillars Further utilitarian measures that were observed were the tiny round speedometer lashed to the left-hand side of the bulkhead, minimal instrumentation in the form of an ammeter, and the speedometer cable, which had a double purpose in that it operated the twin windscreen wipers. At the then current rate of exchange it was supposed the car would sell on the British market for £175 with the possibility of it reducing to under £100 when in volume production.

Despite the economy crisis that engulfed France and its neighbours, of the 1.3 million visitors attending the 1948 Paris Motor Show, thousands of orders alone were taken for the 2CV on the first day, even though production of the cars could not be assured in the short term. Not only were there some fundamental technical details about the car still to be finalised, such as those relating to the engine, the tooling at Levallois had yet to be put into place. When the car eventually entered production on 23 June 1949, its build rate was commensurate with the 2CV's frugal power output. The first production 2CV left Levallois in the first few days of July and thereafter production continued at the lethargic rate of around thirty-five a week, a total of 876 having been constructed by the year's end. Overall, car production in France courtesy of all manufacturers was slow to get going: from just

Constructing the 2CV at Levallois in the early days of the car's production. The poor-quality photograph nevertheless clearly shows the corrugated bonnet being slid into position. (Citroën)

5,000 vehicles being constructed in 1947 when manufacturing restarted after the war, the figure had risen to no more than 20,000 by the end of 1949.

There was an improvement in output at Levallois in 1950 when 6,196 2CVs left the assembly line. Nevertheless, the chance of actually owning a Deux Chevaux was very slim, even if one had placed an order when it was first announced. Most of the early production was destined for export to earn urgently needed foreign currency, and therefore mirrored a similar situation in Britain where the edict was 'Export or Die'. With the huge demand for the corrugated looking Citroën, it can be supposed there was some skulduggery going on with cars changing hands at inflated prices on the black market. There was also some manipulation, where influential customers were able to jump the order queue, a malaise that was duly noted in the French motoring publications of the time. Even with production increasing to 100 cars a week in 1951, and rising substantially in excess of 21,000 the following year, there was no satisfying demand, despite the Levallois factory working at full capacity.

Officially it was only Citroën agents who were allowed to sell the 2CV, with supposed regulations on sales that were based upon a customer's means. Only essential users were justifiably allowed to buy a car, and then they had to prove they were unable to work without one. Hence it was mainly those working on the land as smallholders, country doctors, midwives, priests and veterinary surgeons who were eligible, and moreover had to be vetted by Citroën inspectors to ensure they qualified. Additionally, as a further security, they had to provide Citroën with regular reports on their car's reliability and usefulness.

Keeping pace with output, the price of the 2CV increased, climbing to 283,000 francs in May 1951 and 323,000 the following October, and then to 341,870 francs in the spring of 1952. There was a single colour available, the *gris métallisé*, equalling the grey economic mood of France. Even the wheels were grey to match, and to be correct were officially described as *aluminium*. It is claimed that a special mottled 'dirt-resistant' paint scheme

La 2ᶜᵛ CITROËN *Traction Avant* AU SALON 1948

News of the 2CV's launch at the 1948 Paris Motor Show was widely publicised in the French newspapers. (Henk Schuuring/Citroën)

LA 2 CV CITROËN
Traction Avant

C'est un moyen de transport pratique, confortable et de qualité pour tous ceux qui ont à se déplacer.

C'est une vraie voiture avec 4 vraies places et 4 portes.

Elle transporte 4 personnes et 50 kg de bagages à 60 km/h.

Elle est économique de fonctionnement et économique d'entretien.

Elle consomme, suivant la vitesse, de 4 à 5 litres d'essence aux 100 km.

Le démarrage à commande mécanique se manœuvre du siège du conducteur. Il ne nécessite pas d'accus qui coûtent cher, sont lourds et demandent de l'entretien.

Direction douce à crémaillère.

4 points seulement à graisser.

Toit découvrable.

Son prix serait de : 185.000 francs, sur la base des salaires et des prix en août 1948.

Livraison : Courant 1949.

S'informer auprès des Concessionnaires et Agents CITROËN.

Detail from the initial 2CV brochure. (Citroën)

was once planned, but any firm consideration to this was ditched prior to the car entering production. *Gris métallisé* it was until October 1952 when the shade of grey became a dark gloss – *Gris plus foncé verni* – and at the same time yellow replaced the aluminium wheel colour. The limitations in respect of paint colours available were as much owing to the constraints in paint supplies as the logistics and disruption a choice of colour would have on volume output. It was 1959, a full decade into production, before another colour, *blue glacier* with a blue roof, was specified in addition to the by now standard grey. Two years later, the colour range was expanded to include yellow and green offerings (*le jaune panama* and *vert embrun* respectively).

Despite Citroën's careful rationing to its customers, and the output increasing to some 400 cars a week by 1952, the waiting list nevertheless extended to between eighteen months and two years. The demand for the Deux Chevaux was heightened still further when, in March 1951, a light van, the Fourgonnette, which was given the AU model designation, was added to the catalogue and built alongside the Type A saloon. The sides, roof and twin rear doors with their small oval windows were formed from ribbed panels to keep weight to a minimum while maintaining the required amount of strength. Indeed, its corrugated appearance exemplified perfectly the Fourgonnette's role in French society as being the basic yet extremely affordable and efficient means of transport it proved to be. The added weight of the vehicle, and its 250 kg payload, called for 135 x 400 Pilote Michelin tyres in place of the Type A's 125 x 400, and accordingly the Fourgonnette's performance was, at 60 km/h maximum speed, somewhat tardy compared to the saloon's 65 km/h. Fuel economy was compromised at 5 litres per 100 km instead of between 4 and 5 litres per 100 km. The Fourgonnette was a practical development of the 2CV, its suspension and carrying capacity being ideal for conversion to a small commercial vehicle which became the popular choice for a variety of traders to include market gardeners and light industrialists. In later times a snapshot of any French village or urban street would not be complete without sight of a 2CV van in use by a boulanger, épicier, poissonnier or very often a vitculteur. More essentially, the Fourgonnette became the workhorse of the French postal service. It was also put to use as an ambulance as well as serving with utilities such as Electricité & Gaz de France. Elsewhere in Europe it found favour with the Belgian postal service as well as ANWB, which is the Netherlands' equivalent of the British AA and RAC.

The Fourgonnette was much more than a 2CV chassis with a van body attached to it. It was purposely designed with a stronger platform and greater ground clearance in the interest of the increased load it would carry. The load area was slightly wider and taller than the cab, and it had a flat floor to enhance its carrying capacity, which meant that the spare wheel was moved to a compact compartment positioned forwards on the driver's side ahead of the rear wheel arch. Likewise, the fuel tank was relocated in a similar position on the opposite side of the vehicle.

From the ridicule the Deux Chevaux endured on its introduction, opinions changed when those who so belligerently criticised it were able to sample the car and appreciate its sound design and philosophy. Glowing reports emerged from the media, applauding the 2CV for its soft suspension that allowed it to travel over potholes and bumps with ease and without affecting the composure of its passengers. There came the realisation that the humble machine could out-perform other cars by being driven up and down kerbs at 20 mph as well as traversing what was called bomb-packed *pavé* without compromising the ride quality.

An early production 2CV in use with a boulanger. The roll-back canvas roof and the roll-up boot covering are shown to good effect; in this instance, the rear seat has been removed to enhance the load-carrying capacity. (Citroën)

The double chevrons within the oval surround on the grille identifies this as a first series 2CV. In this delightful family scene, the 2CV's roof has been fully opened, possibly as a means of carrying a large item. (Citroën)

This early 2CV shows some parking scars and appears to be using the wooden pole to secure its forward movement. (Author's collection)

The interior of the early 2CV was bereft of instrumentation. The speedometer is lashed to the offside pillar, with the cable also serving to drive the windscreen wipers. There is no fuel gauge, but when this photograph was taken the 2CV had been fitted with an ignition key and door locks for security. (Citroën)

An early Fourgonnette showing the corrugated body, which was designed to afford its necessary strengthening. The fuel tank has been moved from the rear of the car to behind the cab, the spare wheel being positioned on the opposite side of the vehicle. (Author's collection)

Traction Avant **CITROËN**

LA CAMIONNETTE 250 kg - 2 cv

Commode
Le plancher plat et les portes " armoire " facilitent le chargement. Grande capacité et pas de place perdue.
Suspension extrêmement douce : pas de cahots, donc pas d'emballages compliqués à prévoir.

Économique
Prix d'achat raisonnable. Consommation : à 40 ou 50 km/h de moyenne, 5 à 6 litres aux 100 km.
Entretien facile : 4 graisseurs.

Sûre et confortable
Tenue de route traditionnelle des "Traction-Avant". Freins hydrauliques puissants. Direction à crémaillère.
De la place pour le conducteur. Siège très doux (Possibilité d'adjoindre un siège " passager ").
Bon chauffage en hiver; bonne ventilation en été.

Haute qualité
Technique Citroën : précision de la mécanique, qualité des matériaux, rigueur des contrôles de fabrication.

What customers found was a car that, despite its austere appointment, offered luxury in terms not previously considered. The interior spaciousness defied the car's compact dimensions thanks to the slim doors which were unencumbered by a window-winding mechanism, added to which the material-covered simple rubber-strap hammock seats afforded true support and comfort. Four adults discovered ample leg room by virtue of the cabin's flat floor which was made possible by adoption of front-wheel drive, and therefore the absence of a propeller shaft tunnel. The canvas roof could be conveniently opened part way, as might a sun roof panel, but was all the more essentially rolled fully back in the style of a convertible, as well as allowing a practical method of carrying large and unwieldy shaped objects as might a pick-up vehicle.

The 2CV's performance became to be understood, and notwithstanding a mere 9 bhp and a miserly 375ccs, the flat-twin air-cooled engine was found to pull well at low revs as well as allowing the car to cruise with a full load in third gear, overdrive top being reserved for speeds over 25–30 mph. The ease and smoothness of gear changing with synchromesh on all ratios defied the awkward-looking gear lever sprouting from the bulkhead.

Created as a means of providing essential transport to potential customers who might never have been able to afford a car, the unassuming 2CV quickly became an object of desire, not only to those free spirits and free-thinkers who frequented the bars and cafés of the capital's Left Bank, for whom the 2CV symbolised their bohemian lifestyle, but also the more affluent Parisians who judged it as a status symbol. As the 2CV became more available, so it became as much part of Paris as the city's familiar landmarks, not to mention the hot, noisy brake dust-infused Metro system as well as the distinctive, often ancient and traditionally green autobus, many of which were built by Chauson, Panhard, Renault and Schneider.

In the provinces the 2CV served a mostly rudimentary role, being pressed into service not only as a means of family transport but as a tireless and reliable workhorse. Builders' trucks, delivery vehicles and farmers' wagons taking chickens and pigs to market were common uses, as indeed they could be seen off-road in fields and vineyards performing a myriad of duties. The fact it was so basic was its enormous appeal, just as Pierre Boulanger had envisaged. Ammeter and speedometer were the only instruments, and not even a fuel gauge was provided, and to check the petrol level in the fuel tank nothing more inventive than a dipstick contained in the filler tube was provided. Lights and horn were operated from a single stalk attached to the steering column, and ingeniously the headlight beam angle could be adjusted by a wheeled knob below the simple facia, which was useful in preventing a shaft of light being directed skywards when the car was fully loaded and the tail well down on the suspension. With the speedometer cable affording the means of driving the windscreen wipers, there remained a problem at low speeds, often when climbing hills at a snail's pace, of their lethargy when unable to sufficiently clear the screen. For convenience, and not least safety, a twist-action hand control sufficed. Apart from the accelerator, clutch and brake pedals, a pull-starter, choke, umbrella-style handbrake and the push-pull-and-twist gear lever were the only other controls. The absence of direction indicators, interior lighting, lockable doors and a heater added to the parsimonious appointment of the car, and no one seemed to mind that wind-down windows were not a feature. Instead, the lower section of glass on the front windows (those on the rear doors were fixed) could be left to characteristically flap on their hinges in the breeze and in time with the car's motion. The glass could also be swung outwards through one hundred and eighty degrees and secured in the open position by a simple catch on the top edge of the door, the design remaining untouched throughout the car's production. A full-width flap in the scuttle immediately below the windscreen could be opened via a turn screw to increase the level of ventilation, there being a mesh guard to restrict insects from being drawn into the cabin.

The thrifty nature of the Deux Chevaux was revised in 1950 when it was decided to give the car some security by the provision of an ignition key that also operated the newly specified door locks. The decision to add door locks and an ignition key was arguably made in light of the rising values of used 2CVs and to deter their theft. Little by little, further revisions to the original basic specification were made, though it has to be stated that these hardly detracted from the simple character of the car.

The first significant styling modification given to the 2CV was to redesign the insignia on the grille by removing the oval surround and reshaping the double chevrons slightly. The ripple bonnet remained unchanged. (Citroën)

Similar grille modifications were made to the Fourgonnette by removing the oval surround. The lift-up panel giving access to the spare wheel can be seen ahead of the rear wheel arch. (Citroën publicity, Author's collection)

The first major modification was announced in September 1954 with the introduction of a slightly more powerful engine, the size being increased by 50cc to 425cc and leading to the AZ designation. The Fourgonnette was simultaneously uprated to become the AZU, but both vehicles remained available with the original 375cc motor until 1959. A few months before, the Citroën insignia adorning the bonnet air intake was redesigned with remodelled chevrons that were now without the oval surround. Flashing direction indicators positioned on the windowless rear quarter panels were specified, their design affording both rear and forward illumination from a single bulb in each unit. Modification to lighting included the fitting of two tail lamps instead of a single affair, and additionally incorporated a stop light.

In April 1954, six months before the official announcement of the larger engine, *Motor Sport* reviewed a right-hand drive 375cc 2CV following an eighteen-day test, during which more than 2,000 miles were covered by the magazine's founder, Bill Boddy. Somewhat bizarrely it was stated that Citroën had been experimenting with a 425cc engine but had abandoned the project. According to the statement in *Motor Sport*, the 425cc engine had been proposed solely for the Fourgonnette to give it improved performance, which would certainly have been appreciated at times when the vehicle was loaded to capacity. It was claimed that when news of the plan became known, French owners of 2CVs threatened to acquire the new cylinders, increased in bore from 62 to 66 mm while leaving the stroke and compression ratio at their original 62 mm and 6.2:1 respectively, and fit them to their cars to give them the greater acceleration and top speed, something which Citroën argued would spoil the whole philosophy of the Deux Chevaux.

Provision of the optional 425cc engine gave the 2CV an added 3 bhp, taking it to 12 bhp, allowing a big stride in performance by increasing the top speed to 70 km/h, but without compromising fuel economy to any great extent by affording up to 5 litres per 100 km/h. The extra power was especially welcomed by those customers living in hilly and mountainous regions, as not only did the additional cubic capacity engine make for easier hill climbing, it obviated the need, on some occasions, for passengers to alight from the

On a snowy day in 1953, a Citroën representative, possibly from a dealership, explains the finer points of the 2CV's engine and transmission to an interested audience. (Author's collection)

A post-1953 2CV pictured outside a Citroën dealership. Ahead of the 2CV is a Renault Dauphine, which replaced the Renault 4CV in 1956. The photograph was taken post-1961, as evidenced by the Ami 6 advertisement on the wall of the garage. In the garage compound can be seen a Peugeot and an ID or DS. (Author's collection)

This evocative image of a post-October 1953 2CV with Mont St Michel as a backdrop suitably demonstrates the Citroën's easy-to-live-with style. (Citroën)

vehicle to enable it to ascend a particularly steep incline. It was not unknown on difficult ascents for passengers to have to help push the vehicle on its upward climb.

An interesting development was specification of a centrifugal clutch, the option being available only on AZ models and fitted as standard. The centrifugal clutch, unofficially referred to as the 'trafficlutch', made the 425cc 2CV popular with customers whose driving habits were mainly confined to urban areas. Allowing the clutch to disengage automatically at low speeds not only provided a style of semi-automatic transmission, but also afforded more relaxed and clutch-pedal-free driving in heavy traffic. The centrifugal weights came into action at 1,000 rpm, thus engaging first and second gears on starting the engine in much the same way as if the car had been fitted with a fluid flywheel. On level ground it was possible to pull away in third gear, the torque of the engine and flexibility of the clutch allowing this without stalling. An additional benefit was that it saved on petrol consumption, but the downside was that the car could not be push-started in the event of a flat battery, and since 6V electrical systems were the order of the day, this was not an uncommon situation. 2CVs were of course supplied with starting handles, and a car with a centrifugal clutch could be enticed into life with a swing of the handle. The centrifugal clutch remained a standard feature until 1961, after which it became an optional extra. For those customers opting for the 425cc AZ, the centrifugal clutch proved to be very efficient, especially as at low speeds the car could be allowed to coast, though some vigilance was necessary as extra emphasis on the brakes was necessary since engine-braking was largely eliminated.

Doors on the early 2CVs were hung, and not hinged, on the centre pillars. A year after the grille modification, the size of the engine was enlarged to 425cc to afford 12 bhp, though the original 375cc unit remained available until 1959. (Citroën)

The announcement of the availability of the centrifugal clutch coincided with Renault's announcement that it was offering its 4CV, which in right-hand drive form was marketed as the 750, with a French Ferodo automatic clutch as a £20 option.

Only minor technical revisions, such as specifying a different carburettor and modifying window fastenings, were made until the announcement of the AZLP model in September 1957 for the 1958 model year. There were, however, a couple of interior and exterior styling changes, namely moving the direction indicator switch from the left-hand side of the instrument panel to the centre of the bulkhead, and the provision of a heater, which directed warm air from the engine manifold into the cabin and to the base of the windscreen ahead of the steering wheel. Externally the 2CV was given a larger rear window that was fabricated into the full-length canvas roof and boot cover in order to improve rearward visibility while allowing more light into the cabin. All this prompted the introduction of the AZL, the 'L' denoting luxury, which was announced in December 1956. Other touches of plushness included provision of better-quality seat coverings.

The 2CV's propensity to lean at alarming angles when cornering is shown to good effect with this Swiss-registered car taking a hairpin bend at speed. The muff covering the grille would be fitted in cold weather to aid engine warming and to provide some interior heating. (Author's collection)

This LHD one-piece rippled-bonnet 2CV is among the earliest to survive in the United Kingdom. The car was imported from France some years ago and has the 425cc engine. (Author)

Another view of Ragnar Ragnarson's early 2CV, which is in splendid condition and in daily use. The car is largely original and features the direction indicators on the rear quarter panels, which comprise a single lamp each side and afford both forward and aft illumination. (Author)

Despite its minimal power, the 425cc engine allows for surprisingly good average speeds. Driving this type of 2CV calls for thinking in advance and being in the correct gear to tackle hills. The compliant suspension allows normal bends to be taken at cruising speeds. (Author)

The rear boot covering, rolled up to give access to the car's interior. (Author)

The idea of a luxury 2CV, which was still very basic in comparison to most other cars of the era, had originated in Belgium, where Citroëns had been assembled since 1924, and where 2CV production commenced in 1952. A subsidiary of the French company, formed after the first such enterprise in Britain at Slough (Citroën Cars Ltd), the Société Belge des Automobiles Citroën was established in Brussels at Rue de l'Amazonie in the suburb of Saint-Gilles, but the demand for cars outgrew the premises and a purpose-built factory was built at Forest and opened for business in 1926. Citroëns constructed at Saint-Gilles and thereafter at Forest were mainly destined for home consumption as well as being exported to the Netherlands, Luxembourg and Belgium's overseas colonies. The Forest factory built virtually the same models that were constructed at Levallois but subtly modified for the Belgian market. The factory, which built not only the 2CV but later its derivatives, the Dyane, Ami and Méhari, closed in 1980. The Belgian-built 2CVs of the era up to the mid-1950s were identified by their alloy wheel hub covers and wing spats, and are eagerly sought after by 2CV enthusiasts.

Hammock seats provide exemplary comfort despite their basic appearance. The twist knobs are for hand control of the windscreen wipers, opening the scuttle panel to increase ventilation and, lower left, adjusting the angle of the headlamps according to the weight inside the car and thus the vehicle's angle. (Author)

The simple window fastening mechanism. With the flap lowered, a window flapping in the breeze is all part of the 2CV's eccentric character. (Author)

Don't expect a fuel gauge in an early 2CV. The means of gauging the amount of fuel in the tank is via the dipstick. (Author)

With the arrival of the AZLP in September 1957 came one of the first significant styling modifications of the 2CV. Instead of the canvas roof which extended to the rear bumper, the design was changed so that it terminated immediately below the rear screen, below which a top-hinged metal cover gave access to the boot, and this arrangement remained throughout the car's production. The modification was applied in stages, and for a year the metal boot lid was fitted exclusively to Levallois-built models before being available on all other 2CVs. The exception was with the Slough-built cars, which had a similar modification from the outset of production and which are discussed elsewhere. Negligible changes to the specification were reported for the 1959 and 1960 model years apart from improved heating and de-icing systems along with *blue glacier* as a body colour option, the provision of a radio in the glove tray in front of the passenger and the fitting of 135 x 380 Pilote tyres.

The year 1958 was, however, significant since this saw the introduction of one of the most unlikely cars of all time in the shape of the 2CV Sahara. This derivative will be addressed in greater detail elsewhere, but it must be said that the four-wheel drive 2CV, having two engines – one at the front as normal, the other located at the rear, each mated to a dedicated gearbox and controlled from a single gear lever – was developed entirely for the oil industry.

By now, the 2CV, with its large grille and corrugated one-piece bonnet incorporating side louvres to aid engine cooling, had become a familiar and highly efficient, if fundamental, means of transport. Not only adored by the many thousands of families relying upon it for domestic and commercial purposes, it also enjoyed a wider and more adventurous role. Such was its appetite to travel over the most unfavourable country, and thus fully satisfying its original purpose, it presented itself as the ideal vehicle with which to explore the world. One of the first overland adventures of note was Michel Bernier and Jacques Hugier's 13,588 km tour of Europe's Mediterranean coast in 1952, a trip that was to encompass the Middle East and North Africa at a time when good road surfaces were unheard of there. A year later, Jacques Cornet and Henri Lochon, driving a 375cc 2CV, embarked on a year-long 52,000 km exploration of North and South America, which also included traversing the United States from east to west. Their itinerary en route to

Tierra del Fuego took them to the Bolivian Andes, where they successfully attempted the 17,780-foot ascent of Mount Chacaltaya.

Even more daring was Jean-Claude Baudot and Jacques Seguela's 400-day and 100,000 km drive around the world between October 1958 and November 1959. Leaving Paris, their departure from the Grand Palais was timed to coincide with the Paris Motor Show, their itinerary taking them to Algeria and then south through Africa to the Cape and across the Atlantic Ocean to South America and Rio de Janeiro before heading north to Central America, the USA and across the Pacific Ocean to Japan, Singapore, Thailand, India, Iran and Turkey before crossing into Europe and back to the French capital. In all, they traversed eight deserts and fifty countries while encountering some hostile road and climate conditions. As for the 2CV, it completed the journey on the original clutch, petrol pump and dynamo, which says everything about the car's reliability and durability.

The canvas boot cover was replaced by a metal panel hinged beneath the rear window. The car depicted was photographed in northern France and, like so many 2CVs of its age, shows traffic scars. (Author)

A major styling change came in December 1960 when the original single-piece corrugated bonnet was replaced with a smoother-looking five-ribbed affair along with a new design of grille. The four-light body styling remained. (Citroën)

The new bonnet arrangement was a three-piece affair, the sculpted side panels allowing for efficient cooling for the engine compartment. (Citroën)

Levallois in the 1950s with ripple bonnet 2CVs in production. Relatively few photographs of the interior of Levallois exist, which adds to the factory's, and the 2CV's, enigma. (Citroën)

Citroën was already famously associated with explorative missions in the 1920s and 1930s when its cars, fitted with caterpillar-type tracks employing the Kegresse principle, crossed the Sahara Desert, explored darkest Africa and crossed the divide from east to west, traversing against all odds the Himalayas to arrive at Peking, now Beijing.

Not only for exploration purposes, the 2CV was acknowledged by other car manufacturers keen to see how it was put together and to establish the secrets of its go-anywhere ability. Jaguar was one such company, and having acquired an example to fully examine its technology, employed it as a factory runabout for a number of years. The car was enjoyed by employees who remained impressed as to how much energy could be extracted from something so light and fragile looking. The 2CV's finer points were valued by none other than Rolls-Royce's chief stylist, who drove his 2CV to and from the firm's Crewe offices each day and parked it (with criticism from the company's directors) adjacent to those cars referred to as being the 'Best in the World'.

Possibly the most unusual of all 2CVs was the Sahara, which sported two 425cc engines, one at the front, the other at the rear, to afford four-wheel drive. The Sahara was originally designed for use with the oil industry but was also employed elsewhere thanks to its ability to traverse virtually any surface. (Citroën)

The agility of the Deux Chevaux was exemplified as being the choice of oil companies in French North Africa wanting a lightweight vehicle capable of travelling between oil and mineral exploration sites. The mostly roadless region presented serious challenges in the way of effective transport, and thus Citroën set about devising a suitable vehicle that was exceptionally rugged and able to traverse flat sand, rocky surfaces and near mountainous sand dunes. Citroën engineers did not have to look far to find the basis of what was required since the ensuing machine, albeit designed specifically for the purpose, was a none other than a 2CV modified to afford four-wheel drive. When fully developed, the all-terrain, all-wheel drive Tin Snail was given twin engines and transmissions in tandem to make it the only two-engined 4x4 then in existence. Such was the versatility of the appropriately named Sahara that it could serve either as a normal front-wheel driven 2CV or, with both drive trains engaged, as an extraordinarily adept 4x4.

When introduced in 1958, the Sahara was little more than a basic 2CV with a number of modifications to include a strengthened chassis suitably configured to carry the rear engine and gearbox turned back to front. Front and rear bumpers were reinforced, and fatter 155 section tyres were specified along with protection to the undersides of the engines. The fuel tank, customarily located beneath the rear seat, was replaced by twin tanks, one for each engine and positioned inside the cabin beneath the front seats, the fuel fillers being reached through an aperture in the each of the front doors. Filling the boot space astern of the rear seat, the aft engine could be accessed via the boot panel, which had a round air intake cut out of it. Additional cooling was crucial for the rear engine, this being made possible by the provision of louvres in the rear quarter panels above the rear wings, which, owing to the amount of space the engine occupied, were wider than on normal cars and had cut away lower edges to aid wheel changing. The spare wheel, usually carried in the boot, was moved to sit upon a modified bonnet and secured with straps. With both 425cc engines and transmissions engaged, linkages fore and aft allowed the driver to control the car somewhat normally.

With its 650 kg kerb weight and equal weight distribution, the Sahara's climbing capability was such that it outperformed many purpose-built commercial all-terrain

Access to the Sahara's rear engine was via the metal boot lid. A cut-out allowed for adequate cooling, along with louvres positioned in the rear quarter panels. (Citroën)

Few Saharas survive, this example being sold at auction around 2015. Note the spare wheel carried on the bonnet. The petrol fillers are accessed through the front doors and feed two fuel tanks positioned beneath the front seats. (Author's collection)

The interior of the Sahara showing twin ignition keys – one for each engine – and the floor-mounted gear lever, which could be locked to change the ratios of both gearboxes. The simple seats are shown, under which the fuel tanks are located. (Citroën)

vehicles. Its low weight combined with skinny wheels and tyres plus exceptional traction meant that the Sahara could skilfully cross all difficult surfaces with ease. Steep sand dunes presented little impediment, as did other loose terrain, and tests with the car showed it to be impervious to mud and snow. Moreover, the compliant suspension gave it the ability to cross rocky ground, whereas other vehicles would lose traction.

During development of the Sahara, both engines were fitted with centrifugal clutches, but owing to the nature of the vehicle – and the loss of traction when either engine was running at idling speed – this feature was omitted on production models. Nor did the familiar push-pull gear lever sprouting from the bulkhead make it to the production version, and in its place a specially configured floor-mounted device with linkage connecting to the rear gearbox allowed for appropriate control of both transmissions when running in tandem. The usual mechanical clutch found on standard 2CVs was supplanted by a hydraulic device to better control both gearboxes. Other features specific to the Sahara were a steering lock indicator fitted to the steering wheel to aid navigation over mud and loose sand, and the ability to run on the rear engine only should the front engine's fuel tank become empty.

Production of the Sahara began in 1960 and continued until 1966, during which time 694 examples were built. In fact, 695 chassis were constructed, the last never seeing it to completion as a Sahara owing to the project being terminated, and being converted to a standard 2CV saloon. The car was sold as a dark green AZ, but when examined in later years when it was offered for sale, the chassis modifications and cooling louvres in the rear quarters remained in evidence. A Sahara was also kept by Citroen Cars Ltd at Slough and was often used by Nigel Somerset-Leeke, the firm's Sales and Marketing Manager. Of the 694 Sahara 2CVs constructed, eighty were purchased by Spain's Guardia Civil. Only a few Saharas survive though there are a number of replicas in existence. Needless to say, genuine Saharas are revered by Citroën 2CV enthusiasts worldwide.

The go-anywhere attitude of the 2CV is shown in this evocative photograph of a pre-1965 model carrying a Paris registration. Opening the roof to its full extent gave the 2CV its cabriolet style. (Citroën)

3

The 2CV Matures

The 1961 model year proved to be a watershed in respect of 2CV design when, in December 1960, restyling gave the car an extensively modified frontal appearance. The familiar one-piece ripple bonnet gave way to a smoother-look three-piece affair with five lengthways ribs running along the top panel surface. Beneath the upper bonnet sheet and either side of it, panels with longitudinal ventilation recesses opened into the engine compartment to aid cooling. The new bonnet arrangement would be the face of the Deux Chevaux until production ended in 1990, though changes to the grille, headlight and bumper designs would continue. Instead of the large sixteen-slat grille, the new styling incorporated the double chevrons within a smaller, five horizontal strip air-intake, with its aluminium surround giving the 2CV a sharper and more modern image.

Complementing the 2CV's new look, a revised interior brought improved quality seat covers. Additionally, a choice of vibrant yellow and blue paint options added to the car's appeal. Within months, even more sunny colours to include red, beige green and Monte Carlo blue were added to the catalogue, which helped give the Deux Chevaux an ever-youthful persona. Technical revisions were minimal to include new and stronger door locks which added to the security of the vehicle while addressing the safety of its passengers. The Fourgonnette remained unchanged in its design until July, when it also received the modified frontal treatment.

The new face of the 2CV, while doing little to dramatically transform the original ethos of the car, nevertheless kick-started the gradual introduction of significant developments to include completely new models. The first of these was the AZC 2CV Mixte which, announced in March 1962, also became known as the Combi since it was perceived as a commercial version of the saloon without it employing the Fourgonnette principle. It differed from the basic Deux Chevaux by having what was essentially a tailgate that was hinged above the rear window rather than below it, thus enabling improved accessibility to the car's interior. A means of increasing the load space was affected by provision of a folding rear seat, and accordingly the spare wheel was relocated to sit above the engine in a specially designed cradle so as to be easily accessible.

A few months later, in September 1962, the 2CV's interior was given a radical makeover with the speedometer, which was previously affixed to the windscreen pillar, being incorporated into the small binnacle positioned behind the steering column. Built into it, a fuel gauge dispensed of the dipstick within the fuel tank while electrically operated

This post-1960 2CV has larger overriders. From 1962 the 2CV was given updated instrumentation, with the speedometer being housed within a binnacle ahead of the driver, and at last a fuel gauge was specified. (Citroën)

windscreen wipers were a welcome modification. Slightly increased performance was offered in February 1963 with an uprated Solex carburettor and revised gearbox ratios, these helping to raise the car's top speed to 95 km/h, but at a cost to fuel consumption, claimed at being 6 litres/100 km. Another new model arrived a month later in March 1963 designated as the AZ AM (AM standing for 'améliorée', or improved), which later became known as the AZAM and offered customers more luxury than was otherwise found on the basic AZ. Luxury seems hardly appropriate when describing the Deux Chevaux; nonetheless, it afforded such items as a sun visor for the front passenger, while the driver's sun visor now contained a vanity mirror. Seat coverings of a new design and improved quality gave the AZAM a marginal plushness, but it was stainless steel hubcaps, bright alloy bumper overriders and additional bright trim which included a centre bonnet strip that gave it its more upmarket appearance.

Not even the humble Deux Chevaux was exempt from the raft of safety regulations that were sweeping through Europe during the early to mid-sixties. Other cars sporting the so-called suicide front-opening, rear-hinged front doors, the likes of the Fiat 500 Nuova and its larger 600 sibling, were forced to adopt front doors that were hinged on the A pillars. Thus, the 2CV complied with regulations in December 1964, and at the same time customers could opt to have separate front seats instead of the time-honoured single bench type. Seatbelts also became available, with lap-type mountings for added security. By this time, Citroën, having fitted Michelin X radial tyres to the 2CV in 1960 to replace the original Michelin Pilotes, a move that wasn't surprising since Michelin owned Citroën, and had in June 1964 specified Michelin 125 x 380 Tubeless X radials for the Deux Chevaux, the first car to receive them as standard.

At the same time as the introduction of the AZAM, the AZU Fourgonnette was given a significant facelift with the addition of rectangular windows in the body sides. This was a cue to replace the oval spyholes in the rear doors with rectangular glasses smaller than on the body sides, and a styling modification eliminated the corrugations above the body waistline. These revisions predated the announcement a month later, in April 1963, of a new model of Fourgonnette: bearing the AK350 appellation in acknowledgement of its 350 kg payload and incorporating its predecessor's design changes, the newcomer's additional carrying capacity was achieved by lengthening the body as evidenced by the increased overhang beyond the rear wheels. The vehicle's increased dimensions, weight and carrying capacity called for replacing the 425cc engine with the 3CV 602cc unit fitted to the Ami 6, Citroën's 'medium-class car', which had been introduced in 1961 as a 'super 2CV'. An air-cooled flat-twin having similar design principles to the original 375cc and 425cc engines, the 602cc unit afforded the AK350 its improved performance. Both the AZU and AK350, plus the even larger capacity AK400 with its high roof configuration, remained available until the spring of 1978 when all models were replaced by the Dyane-based Acadiane, which is covered in greater detail elsewhere.

Left: The most significant change to the 2CV's styling arrived in 1965 when a six-light arrangement was introduced. At the same time the front doors were hung on the front pillars to satisfy safety regulations. (Citroën)

This side profile of the 2CV clearly illustrates the new body styling that was introduced in 1965. (Citroën)

Visitors to the Paris Motor Show in October 1965 were treated to the 1966 model year 2CV with its new body styling. To the observant, the new alloy grille with its three instead of five horizontal slats and with the chevrons positioned above the air intake on the bonnet pressing was a minor issue. More striking was the six-light body arrangement with small windows built into the rear quarter panels. Not only did the restyling allow more light into the cabin, it afforded the Deux Chevaux a more modern appearance. Additionally, black plastic padding was applied to the bumper inserts and overriders which, it was claimed, afforded the car greater protection from minor bumps when parking. As anyone who has witnessed the method of street parking in Paris will testify, there's only one way to get into a space less than the length of one's vehicle, and that's to not always gently bump it into position! Technical changes included replacing the simple universal cardan joint drive shafts with fully homocinétique types, and at the same time supplanting the friction dampers fitted to the rear suspension with telescopic hydraulic shock absorbers. Apart from relatively secondary styling revisions, this is the look the 2CV employed throughout the remaining years of its production.

By the end of the 1966 model year, total output of the 2CV had reached the dizzy figure of 2,400,090 examples, that year seeing 168,357 saloons leaving the production lines, the largest number to be produced in any one year. Add to the figure 55,817 Fourgonnettes and 27 Saharas, and the year's production had swollen to 224,201. By any standard this was a huge achievement, and remarkably annual production of all types of 2CV-based vehicles would surpass the figure eleven times in the future. Notwithstanding the original philosophy of the Deux Chevaux serving as economical transport to a particular segment of France's population, its classless image made it the country's most respected car, and one that families from all areas of society desired, either as a primary or secondary vehicle.

Design modifications were made at the same time to the Fourgonnette as the Saloon. This street-worn example with a rope fastening the bonnet was photographed in San Francisco. (Bill Wolf)

Fourgonnettes were put to many uses, as illustrated by this 2CV pictured in Lisbon serving as a mobile sweet shop. The car is a post-1974 model, as indicated by the grille arrangement. (Author)

Giving independence to younger people, it was the choice of students, for whom its down at heel image, especially furnished with parking scars, served as a rebellious statement.

A dramatic drop in 2CV saloon output was recorded in 1967, plummeting by 69,674 vehicles from the previous year to 98,683. Immune from the downturn, the Fourgonnette output remained relatively stable, with only 536 fewer constructed than in 1966. The clue to the dip in production was the introduction of the Dyane, which was viewed as being an upmarket 2CV sharing much of its sibling's technology and components. Though the Dyane is discussed in detail elsewhere, its introduction was well received as illustrated by there being 47,712 sold in its first year. Likewise, during the 1968 model year, 2CV output continued to dive, with 57,473 being constructed, along with 51,545 Fourgonnettes at a time when Dyane production rose to 98,769. The tide turned in 1969 when some 72,000 2CVs were produced, the figure continuing to rise to more than 121,000 the following year.

The three-slat grille on this 2CV photographed for a brochure cover is post-1965. This was the time when a number of editions became available, including the AZAM. (Citroën)

Another minor makeover in April 1967 gave the AZAM export model small rectangular direction indicators fitted to the lower part of the front wings. The interior of the car was also upgraded by featuring the instrument panel shared with the Ami 6. The instrument binnacle was, by comparison to that seen on the home market 2CV, all-encompassing with its large speedometer, fuel gauge, voltage meter and switches for the windscreen wipers. A new chevron-shape steering wheel completed the new look, and this was eventually applied to the deluxe models.

Production of the 2CV continued with minimal modifications until early 1970, when it was given an injection of power courtesy of a new and more powerful engine. From the dip in 2CV sales witnessed in the late 1960s it might be supposed that the Umbrella-on-Wheels was losing favour with customers. The fact is that the development leading to the introduction of the Dyane was all part of the plan that this upmarket 2CV would replace the Tin Snail, which ultimately did not happen. With the 2CV's growing demand in 1969 when production accounted for 72,044 vehicles, output increased in 1970 with 121,096 vehicles, nudging up to 121,264 the following year before dramatically jumping to 133,530 in 1972, all of which was remarkable for a model already thirty years old.

The notion of the 2CV giving way to the Dyane was in evidence in February 1970 when the range of cars was slimmed and consolidated into a choice of just two saloon models, along with the Fourgonnette. Two new engines were made available for the 2CV: the 435cc air-cooled flat-twin which had powered the Dyane soon after its introduction and which replaced the 425cc unit, and the 602cc engine from the Ami 6, the models being marketed as 2CV4 and 2CV6 respectively. The changes had been announced in October 1969, and at

A later model 2CV, post-1974, was photographed in Normandy and has an extended boot, which became a popular accessory. The side flashers at the rear of the bonnet sides were a non-standard item. (Author)

the same time a number of technical modifications were revealed. The pedals, instead of the organ-stop variety, were now of the pendant type; larger rear lights were specified; and in place of the single unit front and rear direction indicators positioned on the rear quarter panels, separate front and rear units improved safety. The rear flashers were incorporated into the modified rear lamp assemblies while circular direction indicators were recessed into the lower edges of the front wings. The instrument binnacle already specified for the export AZAM was fitted, along with a steering wheel embodying a twin-spoke chevron arrangement. For the first time, the 2CV was afforded the luxury of a 12V electrical system complete with an alternator and a 25A.h. battery. Anyone who has owned a 6V 2CV will know all too well the glow worm characteristics of the car's lighting system combined with the vagaries of engine starting with a partially discharged battery.

Despite a mere 10cc difference between the new engine and its 425cc predecessor, the increase in performance was markedly noticeable, the top speed now being 102km/h with the stated fuel consumption of 5.4 litres per 100 km. Nevertheless, there remained some lethargy when accelerating, it taking 23.8 seconds to cover 400 metres from standing under ideal test conditions. The 2CV6 proved to be more athletic by covering the same distance in 22.5 seconds, the top speed being 110 km/h, but fuel consumption was compromised at 6.1 litres per 100 km. Upgrading to the 435cc engine was not entirely about giving the basic 2CV a more exhilarating performance, but more gently prodding it into a world where cars' acceleration and overall speeds were getting keener.

When the AK400 Fourgonnette, also known as the AKS, was unveiled in July 1970, its engine, gearbox, braking, steering and suspension systems were interchangeable with those of the AK350. Its longer body and higher roof, both features that were welcomed by traders appreciating the van's greater carrying capacity, meant compromising performance and economy, the top speed being 85 km/h with 7–8 litres per 100 km fuel consumption.

As well as being popular with commercial customers, the Fourgonnette with its large windows proved attractive to families wanting a small motor home without having to choose a purpose-built caravanette or camper van, such as a Volkswagen Type 2 Transporter. Often, Fourgonnettes converted by their enthusiastic owners could be found featuring all the comforts of purpose-built VWs, Renault Estafettes, Goliaths and DKWs. For those owners less inclined towards inventiveness, Citroën offered a combi version of the AZU known as the Weekend which featured even larger windows on both sides as well as removable rear seats, and it did not take long for resourceful companies to offer the Weekend as a fully fitted camper. A special economy version of the Fourgonnette was made available with the 435cc 2CV4 engine mated to the 2CV6's gearbox, the model being marketed mainly to utility undertakings and were therefore not otherwise generally available.

Had the decline in 2CV production seen in the late 1960s continued, there is little doubt the Tin Snail would have been retired. The resurgence in demand in 1970, which continued throughout the decade to peak at 163,143 units in 1974, the same year seeing the highest sales for the Dyane at 126,854 units, was due to the worldwide oil crisis.

Big cars with their thirsty engines quickly went out of favour, especially in those countries, Britain included, where the threat of fuel rationing led to the issuing of petrol coupons. Car dealerships were overwhelmed with motorists searching for Fiat 500 Nuovas, Renault 4s and Minis. Citroën dealers, too, benefitted by the oil crisis and throughout

Europe generally 2CVs and Dyanes were in high demand. Suddenly their virtues were rapidly appreciated by swathes of customers who had previously disregarded the Deux Chevaux on grounds of it being too basic or weird. Young customers loved it and discovered a whole new meaning to car ownership and motoring. In addition to being economical, comfortable, reliable and wholly functional, the small air-cooled Citroën emerged as a status symbol.

The abrupt rise in demand for the 2CV led to a series of special editions that were designed to maintain interest in the car. The first was the vividly painted orange and white 2CV4 Spot in April 1976, which was followed by the bright yellow 007 in 1981. The 2CV had been given a starring role in the James Bond film *For Your Eyes Only*, and Citroën's marketing people lost no time building on its fame by offering a special edition complete with pistol decals and fake bullet holes. It was followed by the Beachcomber, which was sold in France as the France 3 and acknowledged its country's successful challenger in the 1983 Americas Cup yacht race. Another success was the bright green Bamboo, but none of the special editions enjoyed such demand as the 2CV Charleston with its chrome headlamps and art deco graphics adorning the bodywork, which was offered in striking burgundy and black, yellow and black and two-tone light and grey paint schemes. The Dolly was also popular, and like the Charleston remained available until the end of 2CV production. One of the lesser known variants was the Special E, which was designed to appeal to customers for whom town and city use was the main priority. Truly an economy model, it featured the centrifugal clutch which had been deleted from the catalogue a decade earlier, but sales were disappointingly slow, and it was withdrawn after two seasons.

This charming brochure illustration coincided with the introduction of rectangular headlights in 1974. The type of headlight was not overly popular and was eventually discontinued. At this time the 2CV was made available in the United Kingdom, where it was warmly received. (Citroën)

This rural scene was included in the 1976 2CV, Dyane and Ami catalogue, itself somewhat curious since it made a number of suggestions which today would be seen as being politically incorrect, such as 'Citroën favour front-wheel rather than rear-wheel drive because they are in favour of their cars staying on the road'. (Citroën)

The difference between the design of the 2CV and the Dyane is seen to good effect. Under the skin, both cars were very similar. (Citroën)

The wide cargo space of the Fourgonnette is shown in this Citroën marketing photograph. The model is post-1974, as indicated by the headlights. (Citroën)

Introduced in late 1974 for the 1975 model year, Citroën designers decided to modernise the look of the Deux Chevaux by giving it rectangular headlights. 2CV traditionalists were horrified since the shape of the headlights was at odds with the car's concept, but nevertheless the 2CV continued to sell in healthy numbers. Criticism about the styling must have nonetheless had some impact because, owing to public demand, a back-to-basics 2CV4 marketed as the Spécial was offered for the 1976–77 model year. Not only was a return to the original round headlights made, but the interior was also bereft of superficial finery. The small pod-like instrument binnacle made a comeback, and to please the purists the bodyshell was without its rear quarterlights and the wheels were minus hubcaps. All sorts of rumours abounded about Citroën finding a cache of old-style bodyshells and taking the opportunity to offload them.

The 2CV's new look coincided with the car's return to the British market after fifteen years. The last time the Deux Chevaux had been available on the British market was under the disguise of the fibreglass-bodied Bijou which was unique to the Slough factory and built from 1959, when a prototype was shown, until 1964 when the production line closed.

In the United Kingdom, a demand for used left-hand drive 2CVs was met in the early 1970s when a number of independent Citroën specialists began offering imported cars sourced from France, Belgium and Holland. No doubt the increasing numbers of Britons visiting France and Western Europe discovered the charms of the Tin Snail, and suddenly it became fashionable to be seen driving this French peculiarity. A lucrative enterprise

The arrival of the rectangular headlights corresponded with the global oil crisis. which saw a huge resurgence in the demand for economy cars, resulting in the 2CV finding customers who would not have previously thought about buying a Deux Chevaux. (Citroën)

With high demand for the 2CV in the mid to late 1970s, Citroën introduced the Spécial, which was pared down in price and equipment. Note the return to the four-light body style combined with the latest grille, overriders and direction indicators. The car is without hubcaps to keep the price as low as possible. (Citroën)

In the 1970s a series of special editions were introduced to maintain demand for the 2CV. The first of these was the Spot, which was finished in an orange and white colour scheme. (Citroën)

A particular favourite special edition was the 007, or James Bond version, the car having been used to spectacular effect in the film *For Your Eyes Only*. Fake bullet hole graphics came with the car, which was finished in bright yellow. (Citroën)

materialised on behalf of specialists buying up 2CVs no matter their condition and transporting them to the United Kingdom, where there existed a growing market. The 2CV's popularity ensured the supply of components whatever its age – a situation that remains thus today. While some customers were happy to buy 'as seen' and to renovate cars themselves, others chose to have a 2CV professionally prepared to a useable condition.

The idea of a basic 2CV was a popular move and led Citroën to offer the Deux Chevaux in two trim levels, the Spécial and the deluxe Club version. Externally, both editions shared the same six-light body styling, the Spécial having the rudimentary interior and minimal equipment. By this time technology had caught up with the Tin Snail and both the Spécial and Club gained telescopic hydraulic shock absorbers on the front suspension system. A twin-circuit braking system was adopted, and finally the 435cc engine was dropped from the catalogue, thus leaving the 602cc unit across the range in the interest of performance. Such power, though minimal compared with other small cars, resulted in both models gaining disc brakes, though drums remained at the rear since most braking on a 2CV is achieved via the front wheels, thus leaving the rear brakes doing relatively little work.

Since the arrival of the Dyane into the Citroën catalogue, its upgraded technology was gradually passed on to the 2CV. Whereas the 2CV was expected to go out of production in the early 1970s in favour of the Dyane, the oil crisis had secured its future, and instead the Dyane fell victim to demand, and consequently Citroën's marketing decisions. With its 602cc engine, the 2CV felt remarkably lively compared to its ancestors.

With 101,222 saloons produced in 1979, sales of the 2CV nonetheless went into decline. From 89,994 cars constructed in 1980, within three years the figure had diminished to

A move was made to return to the round headlights, as is seen in this publicity image showing both a rectangular headlight and the latest round headlamp model. The rectangular headlight car is a Club version. Ultimately, all 2CVs returned to having round headlights. (Citroën)

One of the most popular special editions was the Charleston, which remained available until the end of production. Three colour schemes were available: yellow and black, burgundy and black and grey and black. (Citroën)

The Dolly, introduced in 1985, was another favourite special edition, and one which was available until the end of production. By this time, the 2CV sported front disc brakes. Production of the 2CV ended at Levallois in 1988, and thereafter was confined to Mangualde in Portugal. (Author)

Two models of 2CV were marketed: the well-equipped Club and the basic Spécial This is the interior of the Club, showing the instrumentation, which is more elaborate than that found on the Spécial. (Citroën)

The instrumentation of the Spécial features a tiny speedometer and below it a fuel gauge. Switches control the windscreen wipers and washers and a rear fog light. The upholstery is the optional Targa vinyl; on other models it is Jersey nylon. (Citroën)

54,923 in 1984, and to 43,255 by the end of 1987. Sales of the Fourgonnette, which in 1977 amounted to 52,721 vehicles, also flagged, there being 2,535 produced in 1979 as a result of the Dyane-based Acadiane having the greater demand.

Production at Levallois finally came to an end on 29 February 1988, though the 2CV still had life left in it with production moving to Citroën's Mangualde facility in Portugal where models destined for the United Kingdom had been assembled since 1987. The official date of the factory's closure was 29 February, it being a Leap Year, but as a nod to irony, and since this was a Monday, the curtain fell on Friday 26th. Levallois had actually gone into hibernation the day before when the majority of the workforce were paid off. Eyewitness accounts tell of an eerie scenario with the last 2CVs being ceremoniously driven out of the factory, through the open steel gates and along the Quai Michelet. It was not the usual younger drivers who were in charge of the last of the Levallois 2CVs, but the old guard who had known the Deux Chevaux from its ripple bonnet days and who almost lovingly, with respect for history, steered them through the Paris traffic to the waiting car transporters ready to deliver them to designated dealerships.

From the 22,717 2CVs that were produced in 1988, the figure dipped to 19,077 for 1989. Then came the final year for the Deux Chevaux, with a mere 9,954 cars being constructed in 1990 before the production line at Mangualde itself felt silent.

The very last 2CV to be built, a Charleston model, leaves the Mangualde factory in Portugal on 27 July 1990.

The last 2CVs to be built in Portugal comprised the Dolly and Charleston to represent the chic upmarket models. Then there was the Spécial, which was produced in three colours: blue, white and red. For the purists, this was the car to choose with its ultra-basic appointment, the tiny speedometer set into the equally demure binnacle housing a fuel gauge and switches for the windscreen wiper, rear fog light and brake fluid test light. So frugal was its specification that not even an interior light, let alone a radio, was provided.

Look at the last of the 2CVs and compare them to an early model and seemingly little had changed over four decades. What modifications there were over the original specification were mostly discreetly applied, but there's a sting in the tail nevertheless. Portuguese-built 2CVs did not have the same strength of chassis as the Levallois cars, and those examples sent to climates less favourable to those of Portugal, Spain, the south of France and Italy were soon to show signs of deterioration. In addressing complaints from dealers and enthusiasts alike, it became possible to acquire expertly constructed and officially approved galvanised chassis frames. Even three decades after the last 2CV left the production line there is not a single component that cannot be easily and rapidly acquired, which helps to keep the 2CV seen on roads around the world.

Despite production ending in 1990, the 2CV has survived in healthy numbers. One of the last examples to have been built, this car – a Spécial as denoted by the plastic rather than chrome grille – is in regular use. (Author)

There remains a demand for Citroën 2CVs and this garage in Normandy specialises in locating models whatever their condition and either selling them on as seen or renovating them for reliable use. There are a variety of 2CV models seen in this photograph, from late examples as viewed nearest the camera, and an early corrugated bonnet example. Further along the line of cars are examples of Renault 4s, which when introduced in 1961 were set to rival the 2CV and Ami. At the far end of the line of cars a Citroën Type H van can be seen. (Author)

4

The British 2CV

Why and how the 2CV came to be built in Britain must have been questioned many times, especially as it was quite atypical of the type of small car British motorists favoured, and therefore of limited appeal compared to Austins, Morrises and their like. Consequently, the likelihood of it selling in anything other than negligible numbers in the 1950s and 1960s was remote.

In the immediate post-war years, Citroën, despite the marque being perceived as being somewhat unconventional, was nonetheless highly regarded. At the time, the only other car in the catalogue was the acclaimed Traction Avant which, as the four-cylinder Light Fifteen, the wider and longer-bodied Big Fifteen and the latter's six-cylinder sibling, enjoyed a loyal following and were favoured particularly by the motor sport fraternity who recognised the cars' performance and front-wheel drive technology. The Citroën factory located on the huge Slough Trading Estate was already an intrinsic part of the British motor industry, building cars for the home market as well as the British Commonwealth countries. British-built Citroëns had, since the factory's opening in February 1926, enjoyed not only a niche market in the United Kingdom, but also found enthusiastic customers as far away as Australia, New Zealand and South Africa, as well as colonies in East and West Africa and the Indian sub continent.

The decision by Citroën to establish its factory at Slough was largely influenced by the War Office selling land and workshops that had been utilised for the collection, salvage and repair of military vehicles from theatres of war. With the undertaking coming to an end in the early 1920s, by which time many of the retrieved vehicles had been sold on, the facility which had become known locally as The Dump was purchased by Slough Estates, which was formed to provide an important manufacturing amenity. A number of automotive firms had shown interest in moving to the first industrial estate of its type, among which was the Ford Motor Company, though ultimately it decided upon Dagenham.

When under the auspices of the War Office, Citroën had used the The Dump's rough land to demonstrate to the military as well as local authority and corporate companies its Kegresse all-terrain half-track vehicle to good effect. The success of the demonstration proved that not only was the Citroën capable of traversing all types of surfaces, including deep mud and steep banks, but it also received royal approval when Her Majesty Queen Mary was driven over the challenging environment. The Number 3 workshop, the largest of the buildings on the 600-acre site, along with 60 acres of adjoining land for expansion

André Citroën, with spectacles and bowler hat, telling invited guests about the modern technology employed on building his cars at the opening of the Citroën factory located on the Slough Trading Estate in Buckinghamshire. The occasion was the official opening of the factory on 18 February 1926, production at the works having commenced at the end of the previous year. In addition to the rear-drive cars seen here, Slough produced the Traction Avant following its introduction in France in 1934, and after the Second World War built the 2CV and DS models. (Author's collection)

This early publicity photograph of a Slough-built 2CV shows some of the variances between it and the Levallois-constructed cars. The Citroën Front Drive badge on the bonnet was unique to Slough cars; note also the British-built headlights, which differ from the French type, and the semaphore signals fitted to the rear of the bonnet. Slough 2CVs were fitted with opening rear windows, and since the car depicted is without them, this suggests it to be a pre-production vehicle. (Citroën)

purposes, presented Citroën with the ideal manufacturing base. When it was officially opened on 18 February 1926, the vast size of the Citroën factory allowed Citroën Cars Ltd to proclaim it as being the largest car factory under a single roof in Britain. Though the claim was justified, the extent of the manufacturing output would never match that of other British car makers such as Austin, Ford, Morris and Standard.

As far as the British Isles was concerned, Citroëns were well received by customers from the establishment of the marque in 1919. Initially sales of the car were handled by Gastons, the concessionaire also handling a number of foreign makes. With demand outgrowing Gastons' facilities, in 1923 Citroën set up its own headquarters at Brook Green near Hammersmith in West London by taking over the premises previously occupied by International Motors. Growing demand, plus the introduction of a 33.3 per cent purchase tax on imported cars, which became known as the McKenna duty, led to Citroën opening its own manufacturing base so as to avoid the higher tax rate. This was not unique to Citroën since other foreign car makers also opened British assembly facilities, including Renault at Acton in West London and Fiat at Crayford in Kent before moving to Wembley. In order to avoid the duty, car makers had to demonstrate that a substantial proportion of the components were sourced from British manufacturers.

Post-war austerity in Britain and the need to build motor vehicles for export meant that few cars were available to British motorists. Petrol rationing was also an issue, and those customers fortunate enough to buy cars often chose the most economical. With the 2CV in huge demand in France, Citroën Cars Ltd, with the backing of the firm's Paris headquarters, decided that the Deux Chevaux should be built at Slough as soon as volume production of the car was under way at Levallois. Like the Traction Action, the right-hand drive Slough 2CV would also be built in a style that would appeal to British motorists. That the 2CV did not enter production at Slough until 1953 rather than around 1949 to 1950 was owing to British Ministry of Transport regulations, which prohibited cars with inboard brakes being used on Britain's roads. It was only when the rule was relaxed that the tooling and assembly line could be installed.

To comply with the taxation exemption regulations, 51 per cent of the 2CV's components to include electrical equipment, headlights, glasswork, seats, trim and tyres were sourced from British manufacturers. This allowed for the chassis, suspension, engine, gearbox, transmission and body panels to be sent to Slough in kit form. From the outset the 2CV was designed to suit the British clientele, and therefore differed from its French and Belgian counterparts. Adaption to right-hand drive was undertaken at Slough, with the chassis being modified for the steering rack and steering wheel to be repositioned. The accelerator, brake and clutch pedals were relocated, and the speedometer was moved to the centre of the bulkhead.

By far the greatest changes were to the styling and external fittings of the car: instead of the canvas hood seen on French models, Slough 2CVs had an Everflex covering comprising a knitted cotton fabric coated in PVC. Citroën directors in Paris were always bemused by the differences of the Slough cars, both pre- and post-war, over their French cousins, the 2CV being no exception. Not only did they refer to the roof as *la capote anglais*, its design actually pre-dated the modifications made to French 2CVs for 1957. This meant that from the outset of production, the Slough 2CV's fabric roof terminated just below the rear window, which in this instance was larger than that found on the Levallois car,

2CVs at the Slough factory awaiting delivery. The cars have the later type chevrons on the grille, which are minus the oval surround, and DS models can be seen in the background, which dates the photograph to around 1957. A rare 2CV van is seen on the right. (Citroën)

The British-built 2CV was acclaimed by the media and here is a demonstrator, SPP 979, loaned to members of the press. It is seen in the company of a 5 hp at a VSCC rally in 1954 when being tested by the late Bill Boddy for *Motor Sport*. Note the grille muff which was supplied with the car for use in cold weather to aid engine warming. The car is now in the custody of Citroën and is displayed at its museum in Paris. (Author's collection)

and was formed from a plastic material known as Vybak. The Slough 2CV therefore featured a lockable metal boot lid, again pre-dating the 1957 modifications to the French model, and additionally carried a Citroën script badge that was unique to the British car. Semaphore signals were exclusive to the Slough 2CV and were attached to the rear part of the bonnet, itself significantly different with its circular and upright 'Citroën Front Drive' badge destined solely for the 2CV and no other Slough cars. Other variations included half-opening flap-up windows in the rear doors, chrome hubcaps and front bumper overriders while a choice of body colours, namely black, cream, green, maroon and white, were available, as well as the grey seen on French cars.

When the British 2CV came onto the market it was highly acclaimed by the motoring press, and in particular by Bill Boddy of *Motor Sport*. Motoring journalists were fascinated by its utilitarian nature and were impressed by its fuel economy. They accepted that performance, albeit somewhat tardy courtesy of just 375cc, addressed the many problems in running a car during times of austerity. Long expeditions were undertaken to prove the 2CV's stamina and dependability, these including a run in January 1954 from Land's End to John o' Groats courtesy of *The Autocar*, a trip which won the car a high regard. Later on, in 1956, when the 425cc version became available for *The Motor* to test, there was no doubting the 2CV afforded a sensible proposition for a significant number of motorists.

Another view of SPP 979. Bill Boddy subjected the car to an extended tour of Great Britain whereby he amassed more than 2,000 miles in eighteen days. (Author's collection)

The 2CV's dramatic suspension travel is graphically depicted in this photograph taken of a 1955 Slough car loaned to the press for a road test feature that appeared in a Worthing, Sussex, newspaper. The fog light on the near side of the bumper is non-standard. (Author's collection)

Notwithstanding the many compliments aimed at it, the 2CV did not endear itself to the average British motorist, who was unable to appreciate the soft and loping ride, the push-pull gear change and the chattering of the air-cooled twin-cylinder engine. It was marginalised as an awkward foreign car, its front-wheel drive summoned suspicion, and its handling and driving characteristics were misunderstood. As for the interior appointment, it was branded as being bizarrely primitive. British motorists' antipathy towards the 2CV is reflected in there being only 673 examples constructed at Slough during the years between 1953 and 1960, of which 340 were exported to Commonwealth countries, mainly Australia.

Slough produced two commercial 2CV variants, a van and a pick-up, of which a total of 577 were built. Of these, 215 were sold to British customers, the remaining 362 being exported. Though the Fourgonnette proved to be popular in Europe, British customers wanting a small van shunned it in preference to traditional home market brands. A role that the 2CV van successfully provided was, when employed by Citroën Cars Ltd, to make regular weekly trips from Slough to Paris to collect essential components needed to keep vehicle production running. The pick-up version was unique to Slough, the biggest customer being the British Government when in 1959 it ordered sixty-five for use with the Ministry of Defence to be employed by the Royal Marine Commandos. The role of the vehicles was in helicopter lifts in Aden, Borneo and Malaya from HMS *Albion* and HMS *Bulwark*. Trials with the 2CV pick-up had proved successful when the vehicles, which were dropped by helicopter, were able to provide Marines with rapid advance inland transport from a beachhead.

The fate of the 2CV was decided by Nigel Somerset-Leeke, whose appointment as Citroen's UK Sales Manager was confirmed in November 1958. Within two days of him arriving at Slough he was reappointed General Sales Manager and General Publicity Manager with direct responsibility to the firm's Managing Director, Louis Garbe, himself answerable to Paris for all that happened at Slough. Nigel Somerset-Leeke spent his formative years with Morris, having joined the company in 1936 as a young man. A chance sighting of an advertisement in *The Daily Telegraph* prompted him to apply for the position at Slough, only to discover he was one of 200 applicants. After a series of interviews as well as a visit to Citroën in Paris, he was successful in the appointment. One of his first thoughts was that Citroën Cars Ltd should shake off the 'beard and sandals' image which, he had decided, the

Sales in Britain of the 2CV were slow, which isn't surprising considering the car's idiosyncrasies and that British motorists chose the Morris Minor, Austin A30 and small Fords. An attempt to boost demand for the Citroën was to replace it with the Bijou, which was unique to the Slough factory. Under the glass fibre body of the pre-production model, seen at the introduction of the car in 1959 at a special event within the factory, the underpinnings and running gear were totally 2CV. The car on the left of the photograph is a Citroën DS, which was also built at Slough. The Bijou's small air intake was replaced by a larger type to aid engine cooling. The idea of the Bijou came from Nigel Somerset-Leeke, the firm's Sales and Marketing Manager. (Citroën)

company had unfortunately attracted. His vision was to take Citroën wholly upmarket in the semblance of the golf club set and perceived that Citroën should be viewed much in the same way as Jaguar. In his opinion there was no place for anything as primitive as the 2CV, which at the time shared the catalogue with the expensive and technically advanced DS19 and ID19 models with their bristling technology and wildly futuristic styling. Moreover, with such poor sales of the 2CV, the Slough factory was in essence producing the car for stock, of which many unsold examples were stored around the works.

Having convinced Louis Garbe to gain permission from Paris to discontinue the 2CV, Somerset-Leeke set about finding a well-appointed small car. This was, after all, an era of growing prosperity; the age of the two-car family had arrived and the search was on for a chic vehicle which would serve as a quality 'second car' that was ideal for shopping trips and transporting children to and from school. It would carry status and be admired socially. Nothing existed in the Citroën range to match the required criteria, and though Panhard had come under the Citroën umbrella in 1955, for which Slough had the responsibility for marketing in Britain, its unconventional design deterred all but the most adventurous motorists.

Nigel Somerset-Leeke's search for a car that would appeal to a more discriminating customer was therefore focussed on the 2CV. What was needed was a fashionable body styling with an interior appointment to match. Initial thoughts were to produce a baby DS, but producing the car had to be confined to Slough without resource from Paris. The concept, which emerged as the Bijou, was only ever considered for the British market and was therefore unique to the Slough factory. Somerset-Leeke had definite ideas about the

One of the last Slough 2CVs leaving the factory. Behind it are three Bijou models, the car's design largely influenced by the shape of the DS. (Citroën)

THE
UNIQUE
CITROEN
BIJOU

Above and below: Front and rear covers from the Bijou brochure, which clearly markets the car to motorists who would not have previously considered buying a 2CV. Peter Kirwan-Taylor, who styled the Lotus Elite, was commissioned by Citroën Cars Ltd to design the Bijou, its cues clearly being influenced by the expensive, luxurious and radical DS. (Author's collection)

Bijou's styling and design, which by necessity employed the 2CV chassis and engine. The styling was entrusted to Peter Kirwan-Taylor, the young accountant turned car designer who had sculpted the Lotus Elite, and whose work involving that car's fibreglass reinforced polyester resin body construction was already legendary. In the knowledge that Citroën Cars Ltd had neither the manufacturing facilities nor the financial resource to produce steel body pressings for the car, and that it was not viable to approach Pressed Steel owing to the anticipated low-volume production, the agreed course was to have the bodyshell, like that of the Lotus, constructed from fibreglass.

Peter Kirwan-Taylor's silhouette for the Bijou took styling cues from the DS with its roofline, curved windscreen and slim pillars, along with a large glass area and distinctive rear profile. The engine fitted to the Bijou was the 2CV's 425cc air-cooled unit and, given the Bijou's additional weight over the Deux Chevaux, performance was always going to be compromised. Somerset-Leeke had asked to use the exceptional 845cc air-cooled twin from the Panhard PL17 but approval from Paris was denied.

The construction of the fibreglass body was entrusted to a local firm, James Whitson of Cowley Peachey near Uxbridge, a company well-versed in producing fibreglass cabs for commercial vehicles. Owing to manufacturing difficulties, the contract was eventually transferred to C. F. Taylor Plastics of Crowthorne in Berkshire. The Bijou went into production in June 1959, the tooling being supervised by Slough's Chief Engineer, Ken Smith, who had been instrumental in the preparation of the DS and who had spent months in Paris working alongside the car's design team. Three prototype cars were running by the autumn in readiness for the Bijou's debut at that year's London Motor Show. When unveiled at

Bijoux leaving the Slough factory. The car was well received by the media, but despite an encouraging rush of sales, demand diminished partly because of its price, partly owing to its 2CV technology and mainly because of competition from other small British market cars, particularly the Mini, which made its debut at the same time as the Bijou. (Citroën)

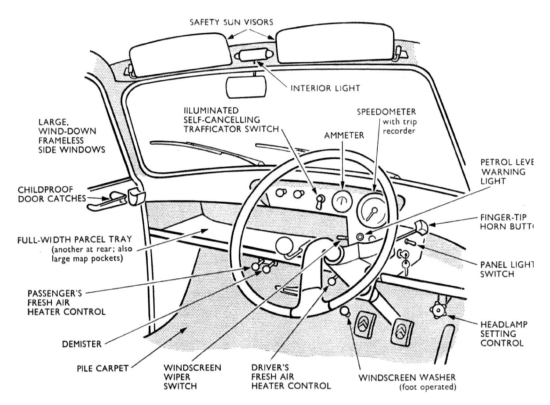

SAFETY SUN VISORS

INTERIOR LIGHT

ILLUMINATED
SELF-CANCELLING
TRAFFICATOR SWITCH

SPEEDOMETER
with trip
recorder

AMMETER

LARGE,
WIND-DOWN
FRAMELESS
SIDE WINDOWS

PETROL LEVE
WARNING
LIGHT

CHILDPROOF
DOOR CATCHES

FINGER-TIP
HORN BUTT

FULL-WIDTH PARCEL TRAY
(another at rear; also
large map pockets)

PANEL LIGHT
SWITCH

PASSENGER'S
FRESH AIR
HEATER CONTROL

HEADLAMP
SETTING
CONTROL

DEMISTER

PILE CARPET

WINDSCREEN
WIPER
SWITCH

DRIVER'S
FRESH AIR
HEATER CONTROL

WINDSCREEN WASHER
(foot operated)

Detail taken from the Bijou handbook showing the car's controls. The single-spoke steering wheel was shared with the DS, and note the 2CV gear change arrangement. (Citroën)

A Bijou showing signs of wear and tear and offered for sale in the late 1990s. Initially selling for £695, its price was slashed to £599, then to £493, and in April 1963 to £433. By the end of the year it had vanished from the catalogue and production ceased in August 1964 after 211 examples had been built. (Author)

Earls Court the Bijou was well received, with customers liking the similarity with the DS and approving the wide range of colour schemes to include Coral Pink, Daffodil Yellow, Dove Grey, Regal Red and Sherwood Green. In contrast to the 2CV, the interior was appealing with its pile carpeting and wind-down windows, though close examination revealed 2CV origins in respect of the push-pull gear lever sprouting from the facia and the umbrella-type handbrake.

Priced at £695 inclusive of purchase tax, the Bijou, compared with some other small cars, was expensive. The basic Mini and Ford 100E Poplar were cheaper by £200 while the Morris Minor and Fiat 600D undercut the Bijou by substantial margins. Renault's Dauphine and the Hillman Minx Special were dearer by merely £20. Nevertheless, the interest in the Bijou was sufficient for Citroën management to approve production rate of thirty cars a week, a figure fourfold the number of 2CVs produced at Slough. The Bijou was also well received by the media, which gave the car encouraging reviews. Both top speed and fuel consumption were better than those of the 2CV, though overall acceleration and performance were marginally compromised because of the car's greater dimensions and additional weight.

Optimism turned to pessimism when demand for the Bijou diminished, and this was not helped by the introduction of the Mini. The price was slashed from £695 to £599, being reduced still further to £493 and later dropped to £433. By the end of 1963 the car had disappeared from the catalogue and in the following August the last example left the Slough factory, the production amounting to a mere 211 cars.

The 2CV van was built at Slough, but unlike in France and Belgium, where demand was high, few British customers were attracted to it. This was at a time when many British motorists were still wary about buying foreign vehicles, even if they were built in Britain. Even accolades such as 'Eye-opening performance' and 'One of the truly great modern designs' could not influence commercial motor customers. (Author's collection)

5

The Variants

Though the 2CV and its bigger sibling the revolutionary DS, probably the most technically advanced car in the world in 1955 and a design leader for generations to follow, there was nevertheless a big gap in the car maker's catalogue. Until 1957, and two years earlier in Britain, the Traction Avant arguably offered the ultimate in comfort and performance. Whereas in the mid to late 1950s other manufacturers sported at least one mid-size family car catering for a broad market, Citroën's shop window was completely bare. While this had not been a problem to Citroën earlier in the 1950s, by the end of the decade the car maker was losing out to rival companies.

Citroën's solution to finding a mid-size family car came in the design of the Ami 6, which was introduced in 1961. In full Citroën spirit it was as idiosyncratic as might be expected. Its styling the work of Flaminio Bertoni, the Ami 6 can easily be classed as one of the most distinctive and unconventional cars to have been produced, and on occasions has been judged the ugliest car ever. A roomy four-seater, it nevertheless shared the 2CV's hypothesis by adopting its chassis and running gear, albeit slightly modified for the enhanced dimensions and increased weight over the Deux Chevaux. On its debut in April 1961, Citroën described its newcomer, with its deeply sculpted bonnet incorporating distinctive 'eyebrows' over the rectangular headlights, gaping mouth air intake and reverse-rake rear window, as the world's most comfortable medium-class car.

The reverse-slope rear window was deliberately chosen by Bertoni to provide the Ami with an elongated flat roof in order to afford as much cabin headroom and interior space as possible. It had the advantage of providing for a capacious boot as well as keeping the rear screen dry and clean in wet weather. A close look at the interior revealed that the design department had raided the DS parts store for door handles, switches and the single-spoke steering wheel. Externally, weight-saving measures included the use of aluminium for the bumpers, front grille and minor trim items. Initially, in common with the DS and ID, the Ami 6 was fitted with a translucent fibreglass roof until replaced by a steel item. Simplicity, as well as keeping weight to a minimum, called for sliding windows in the front doors, and while those in the rear doors at first comprised fixed glass, they were soon supplanted by similar sliding types. The body design allowed for a flat floor and wide bench seats, and with the curved windscreen afforded hugely improved interior space over the 2CV.

In order to provide for adequate performance, the Ami 6 received a more powerful version of the air-cooled twin-cylinder engine, increased in capacity to 602cc to provide

The Ami 6 was introduced in April 1961 as Citroën's mid-size car to fill a gap in the catalogue. Using the 2CV's chassis, the Ami 6 was in effect a super 2CV providing a spacious family car between the basic Deux Chevaux and the luxurious DS and ID models with their highly advanced technology. The scene depicts the launch of the Ami 6 with a drive through of cars in Switzerland. The reverse-rake rear screen afforded the maximum possible cabin space and headroom. Note the early DS19 parked against the kerb on the left of the picture. (Author's collection)

The Ami 6 was often said to be the ugliest car ever made, which unfortunately overlooked the car's many qualities, not least the spacious comfort it afforded. The Ami's underpinnings are entirely 2CV, but to compensate for the heavier and larger body a more powerful twin-cylinder air-cooled engine was specified, the cubic capacity being 602cc. (Author)

Flamino Bertoni's styling for the Ami 6 was distinctive while being wholly functional. The lighting used was at the time the very latest and best available. The car at the rear is the top range Club model, which is identified by its twin headlights. (Author)

22 bhp at 4,500 rpm. This gave the car a top speed of 65 mph without compromising fuel economy and, importantly, gave the car truly comfortable long distance driving ability. Nevertheless, an increase in power to 26 bhp was made in September 1963, raised two years later to 32 bhp to afford 70 mph flat-out cruising. The push-pull gear lever remained, as did the option of a trafficlutch, both being favoured Citroën features. Despite its unorthodox appearance, French motorists loved it, and within a year of its debut it was being produced at the rate of 600 a day at the newly built Rennes-le-Janais factory. Three years later the Ami was outselling the 2CV, such was its popularity as a family car, and indeed second car, often the choice of female motorists. That the car encompassed all the familiar 2CV qualities added to its appeal in respect of reliability and easy maintenance.

On the road, the Ami 6 with its suspension borrowed from the 2CV offered the softest ride while maintaining superb stability, roadholding and handling. Easy to park with its tight turning circle, it became the essential town and country vehicle without losing any of the ethos that went into devising the 2CV. A huge boost in the Ami's popularity arrived with the introduction of the Estate (Break) version in 1964 which offered 53 cubic feet of space and a 660 lb payload, not to mention the aesthetically pleasing revised rear styling which included a fully opening tailgate. Other additions to the Ami 6 range were the availability of a Confort grade trim level in addition to the basic Tourisme. The Confort model featured jersey nylon upholstery instead of vinyl, which while being more comfortable was at risk of deterioration, especially when exposed to long periods of hot sunshine. From 1967 6 volt electrics gave way to a 12 volt system and an alternator, while equipment upgrades included real-world heating and ventilation and windscreen washers. A Club version of the Estate, identified by its twin circular headlight arrangement and upmarket interior arrived in May 1968, the same modifications being applied to the saloon five months later.

A restyled Ami was introduced at the Geneva Motor Show in March 1969. The Ami 8 retained its predecessor's 602cc flat-twin air-cooled engine and general chassis layout, though the body was given a major makeover. The deeply sculpted bonnet gave way to a smoother shaped affair, thus the headlights lost their hooded appearance while the 'face' of the car was tidied. The saloon lost its reverse-rake configuration to a sloping tail but without a hatchback. Six months later the Ami 8 Estate was introduced in two trim levels, the Club having greater luxury in terms of appointment and equipment. At the time of the Ami 8 Estate's launch all models were upgraded to front inboard disc brakes. The Ami 8 saloon remained in production until early 1978, but the Estate was sold until 1979.

Restyled in time to be shown at the 1969 Geneva Motor Show, the Ami, now renamed Ami 8, retained the 602cc flat-twin engine. Styling modifications included a reshaped front while losing the reverse-rake rear screen. The model depicted here is the Estate with its full-height tailgate. All Ami 8 models featured front disc brakes, the Saloon remaining in production until early in 1978 while the Estate continued for another year. (Citroën)

Sharing the Ami 8's styling, the Ami Super as seen here was fitted with a 1,015cc flat-four air-cooled engine originally specified for the Citroën GS. With its larger engine and light weight, the Ami Super boasted formidable performance. (Citroën)

This publicity photograph portrays the Ami Super's high performance courtesy of its air-cooled flat-four 1,015cc engine. Unlike the Ami 8, with its push-pull gear change, the Super was given a floor-mounted change. (Citroën)

Essentially out of the scope of this book, the Ami Super, employing a largely modified chassis, was powered by the 1,015cc flat-four air-cooled engine from the recently introduced Citroën GS sports saloon. Overpowered with formidable performance and an 87 mph top speed, the car remained in production for three years and was halted in late 1976 after 42,000 examples had been built.

The Ami 6 was not constructed at Slough since demand for the car in Britain was nowhere as high as in France and Belgium. With the introduction of the Ami 8, sales in the United Kingdom in both trim levels increased, partly through the popularity of the Citroën marque generally, and because British customers had become more used to seeing this very Gallic car on their travels throughout Europe.

The car that Citroën intended to replace the 2CV made its debut in August 1967. Designed by Louis Bonnier who had created some of the most stylish Panhard cars before the marque was acquired by Citroën in 1953, the Dyane was built on the 2CV chassis and running gear. Combining all the positive features of the 2CV, it went further in provision of a slightly wider but stronger – and therefore heavier – body with modern styling without losing the design ethics of the car introduced in Paris nineteen years earlier.

The family resemblance between the Dyane and 2CV was immediately obvious despite the former's more angular shape with slightly concave doors, headlights built into the integral wings and a full-height tailgate much in the idiom of that seen on the Renault 4. The full-length fabric roof was retained while inside the cabin a new facia layout incorporating the familiar gear change lever gave a sense of more spaciousness. Front windows were of the sliding type seen on the Ami, but those at the rear had fixed glass.

Designed to replace the 2CV, the Dyane was introduced in August 1967, and while the family resemblance with the 2CV is obvious, it was nevertheless more upmarket with its more modern styling which incorporated a full-height tailgate. Early models, as depicted here, were without rear quarterlights, and were powered by the 2CV's 425cc engine mated to an Ami 6 gearbox. Within a year the 425cc engine was superseded by the 435cc unit. (Citroën)

When the Dyane 6 with its 602cc engine was introduced in January 1968, it was given rear quarterlights, as can be seen in this publicity image dated 1969. The 435cc engine remained available for the Dyane 4, which had restricted popularity owing to its limited performance. (Citroën)

The 2CV's 425cc engine, mated to an Ami 6 gearbox, featured on the first Dyanes but within a year the 435cc was specified when the car was given the Dyane 4 appellation. The reason was that in January 1968 a higher-powered version was launched with the Ami 6's 602cc engine, the model being known as the Dyane 6. The Dyane's body was originally a four-light affair, but the Dyane 6 on introduction was given rear quarterlights, the feature expanding to the Dyane 4 in March 1968. There were a number of engine modifications to the Dyane 6, which quickly became the more popular of the two models. In September 1968 the 602cc engine from the 2CV6 was fitted, and in February 1970 it received the Ami 8 engine for improved performance and fuel economy.

Stability and handling were the Dyane's strength, and like the 2CV and Ami it could display alarming angles of tilt when cornering at speed. It was, like the 2CV, basically appointed but had sculpted door cards formed from lightweight plastic to match the facia. There was also rudimentary soundproofing in the form of a compressed paper felt material, and like its siblings the seats could be easily removed for picnic purposes or to increase the luggage space. There were minor styling changes over the Dyane's production to include the positioning and shape of the door handles, the tailgate locking mechanism and the design and material employed for the front grille. Early models had the option of the centrifugal trafficlutch but this was later withdrawn. The spare wheel was initially placed in the boot well but was later relocated to sit above the engine in order to afford greater carrying capacity.

Two trim levels, the basic Luxe and the better appointed Confort, were available, while a choice of a front bench or separate seats existed. There was also a Weekend model featuring a folding rear seat and a platform covering the well in the boot.

With the arrival of the Dyane in the United Kingdom in 1968, customers could again get the next best thing to a 2CV without having to acquire a left-hand drive import. In the time between the Slough 2CV, and Bijou, being discontinued, the demand for the Dyane had greatly increased, partly through the desire to buy ultra-economical cars and partly because the air-cooled Citroëns had achieved a near-cult status. Those customers who dared own a Dyane soon discovered its charms.

Special editions of the Dyane were offered; the first was the Caban, followed by the Capra which was sold in Spain and Italy. A popular edition, the Côte d'Azure was well received both in France and Britain. However, despite, all expectations that the Dyane would outsell and replace the 2CV, these were unfounded. The originality of the 2CV, and its hugely popular following nevertheless, was its saviour and the Dyane in 435cc form was discontinued in 1975 to leave the Dyane 6 in production until 1984. The Dyane concept lingered on with the Acadiane until May 1987, by which time the Peugeot-based Citroën Visa with its 652cc air-cooled twin, introduced in October 1978, found a measure of demand.

A number of variants, usually very low volume, were built for markets requiring an easy to build and inexpensive vehicle. None were more commendable than the Mehari, which was an affordable Jeep-type with a 2CV chassis and Dyane 6 running gear plus a lightweight, flexible open body formed from ABS thermoplastic. Initially built by the SEAB company at Villejuif in France, production was transferred to the Panhard works at Ivry. Never available in Britain, the Mehari was used by farmers and industrialists wanting a no-frills utility vehicle, and there was even a 4x4 version identifiable by its spare wheel carried on the bonnet.

Above and below: Early Dyane models can be identified by a metal grille and upright door handles, as depicted in the right-hand drive example, seen with its hood open as far as the roof's central strut. Later cars had downward type door handles and rear bumpers with their black inserts.

The Dyane became the basis of the new-look Fourgonnette, which replaced the 2CV version. Different styles were available including the Mixte with its rear seats. (Citroën)

The Acadiane proved to be popular with traders wanting a capacious multipurpose van. The hatch below the window gives access to the spare wheel, the fuel tank being positioned on the opposite side of the vehicle. (Citroën)

The Mehari with its ABS thermoplastic body proved to be a rugged choice for customers wanting a versatile lightweight vehicle. Its running gear was wholly 2CV and it became a vehicle often seen in use with farmers. It was also a familiar sight at tourist resorts, but was never imported to the UK owing to its body construction. (Citroën)

The construction of the Mehari was simple insomuch that it comprised thirteen panels, to include the floorpan and wheelarches along with the side panels, optional doors, bonnet, dashboard and tailgate, all of which were riveted or screwed as specified to the tubular steel framework. Initially only the canvas roof and side screens were supplied by Citroën, the optional hard top being supplied by ENAC, a French company specialising in ABS materials. Unlike the Sahara, which had two engines, the 4x4 Mehari had a single engine which was front-mounted with a conventional transfer reduction gearbox thus providing the drive to the rear wheels via a propshaft to allow for seven forward speeds plus a differential lock for traversing particularly challenging terrain. Though a mere 1,313 4x4 Meharis were built to satisfy normal sales, the French Army ordered 5,000 examples in 1981, though these were steel-panelled rather than being constructed from ABS, and were powered by the air-cooled 652cc engine otherwise fitted to the Citroën Visa. Overall, a total of 144, 953 Meharis were built.

The Mehari 4x4, with its all-road traction, skinny wheels and tyres and light weight, proved to be a good off-road performer. Note the spare wheel carried on the bonnet, a relic of the 4x4 2CV Sahara. (Citroën)

This Citroën publicity rendering suitably depicts the Mehari's go-anywhere potential. (Citroën)